Dating 3.0

Finding **LOVE** in the age
of social media
and the smart phone

Dating 3.0

Finding **LOVE** in the age of social media and the smart phone

ANTONIO BORRELLO, PHD
THERESA PAVONE, PHD

Dating 3.0: Finding Love in the Age of Social Media and the Smart Phone

Copyright © 2016 by Antonio Borrello and Theresa Pavone

All rights reserved. No part of this publication may be reproduced, distributed, or transmitted in any form or by any means, including photocopying, recording, or other electronic or mechanical methods, without the prior written permission of the publisher, except in the case of brief quotations embodied in critical reviews and certain other noncommercial uses permitted by copyright law.

This book is not intended as a substitute for the medical advice of physicians. The reader should regularly consult a physician in matters relating to his/her health and particularly with respect to any symptoms that may require diagnosis or medical attention.

Although the authors and publisher have made every effort to ensure that the information in this book was correct at press time, the authors and publisher do not assume and hereby disclaim any liability to any party for any loss, damage, or disruption caused by errors or omissions, whether such errors or omissions result from negligence, accident, or any other cause.

Some names and identifying details have been changed to protect the privacy of individuals.

Manufactured in the United States of America

ISBN: 978-0-692-79469-2

This book is dedicated to our children, Gianna Marie and Antonio Joseph, who have taught us what it means to love unconditionally.

CONTENTS

PREFACE 9

INTRODUCTION 13

SECTION 1

1: BECOME YOUR OWN CUPID 23

2: YOU ARE HERE 33

3: "AM I READY TO DATE, OR NOT?" 49

4: GETTING RELATIONSHIP-READY 69

5: GETTING TO HAPPINESS FIRST: A SIX-STEP PRESCRIPTION FOR EMOTIONAL HARDINESS 85

SECTION 2

6: DATING 1.0 MIXING AND MINGLING 101

7: DATING 2.0 AND BEYOND 107

8: DATING APPS: THE NEXT GENERATION 143

9: BUILDING INTEREST AND ATTRACTION 155

10: THE FIRST DATE 165

11: FIRST DATE FOLLOW-UP 177

SECTION 3

12: DATING AND NEW RELATIONSHIPS 185

13: PLAYERS AND CHEATERS 203

14: CAN FLIRTING BE HARMLESS? 209

15: JEALOUSY, MANIPULATION, CONTROL
AND ABUSE. 215

16: DECIPERING THEIR CHANGE OF HEART 221

17: SO YOU'VE BEEN GHOSTED: HERE ARE
SIX STEPS TO DEAL WITH IT 225

18: DATING AND RELATIONSHIP RULES. 231

SOME FINAL WORDS FROM ANTONIO 247

SOME FINAL WORDS FROM THERESA 251

ABOUT THE AUTHORS 253

PREFACE

Marriage Jeopardy: What is a Divorced Marriage Counsellor Joining Forces with Ex-Wife to Pen Revolutionary Dating Book? What is 'Dating 3.0', of Course!

It may sound strange, unlikely, or even absurd. But it's true—I'm a divorced relationship therapist and psychologist who has teamed up with my ex-wife to write a book about finding lifelong love in our new world of social media and online dating, Tinder and Hinge, texting, Snapchat, Facetime, and the countless other forms of computer-mediated communication that we depend on today.

What may sound even stranger is that together, Theresa and I are more qualified than anyone else to write such a game-changing resource. We are both psychologists who have spent most of our lives helping people improve their relationships at home and in the workplace. We have also taken our relationship full circle—from dating to engagement, marriage, children, separation, and through divorce. And most recently, we have had to rediscover and relearn the whole dating process, this time with the help of modern technology—texting, getting asked out on Facebook, setting up online dating accounts—all the excitement and craziness the digital age can possibly offer.

But why did we write a book together? Some history…

As a psychologist and relationship therapist, I have spent the past fifteen years working with thousands of people to improve and heal their most important relationships. My psychological background and passion for helping people also led me to become a recognized dating and relationship expert. It even inspired me to begin writing my first book.

But then I got divorced.

A divorced relationship therapist! The irony of this situation struck me like lightning. Suddenly, I was forced to reevaluate every aspect of my personal life and professional practice. Was I the relationship expert I thought I was? Did I really know as much about interpersonal relationships as I led myself to believe?

On top of my internal conflict, the divorce was taking a toll on my family. Theresa and I were constantly fighting and arguing about property, parenting time, and everything under the sun. Like most divorcing couples with children, we certainly struggled through a difficult adjustment period, and things weren't good.

But married or not, I think we were both determined to redefine our relationship and successfully uncouple. Through patience, understanding, hard work, and a little bit of luck, Theresa and I were able to develop a new co-parenting friendship that is mutually rewarding and beneficial to our children. And eventually, we also began to think about meeting new people and dating again.

We have both spent the past three years relearning the dating game, a game that has radically changed. Dating is certainly not what it once was just ten years ago. When I met Theresa, social media, smart phones, and texting didn't even exist! Tinder, mobile dating apps, online dating—all of these have changed the dating scene irrevocably. And it can be very challenging if you don't know the rules.

Suddenly, I had an entirely new topic to add to my book.

But still, as I was working on this relationship book I couldn't help but feel like I had a credibility issue. I had lost my voice. Imagine trying to write an authoritative book on relationships right after getting a divorce. I just couldn't seem to get it done.

Then I had a realization.

Theresa and I were great at being friends and co-parents. In fact, our relationship as divorced parents was better than ever. And both of us were in the process of dating again and dealing with many firsts. That's when I realized that I needed to write this book with Theresa. If we could work together to co-author a book about dating and relationships, we would certainly demonstrate how much we believed in and practiced what we preach.

We grappled with some primitive, powerful feelings as we shared stories and compared notes. Somewhere in there, we realized that we'd uncovered unique dating perspectives that could save others from so much frustration and hurt. Combining our psychological background, our unique perspective as a divorced couple, and the new rules of online and mobile engagement, we were able to discover dating strategies that can help anyone searching for love today.

I've had a few people ask me if it was weird to write a dating and relationship book with my ex-wife. If you thought it was hard trying to write an authoritative book on relationships after going through a divorce, try and imagine the "Mission: Impossible" nature of writing this book with a co-author who also happens to be the ex-wife in question! So was it difficult? Yes! But weird? Not really.

Indeed, we disagreed, argued, and struggled . . . but I don't think I could have finished the book without her. For me, nothing is more important than my relationships. My whole career has been focused on helping people to save their marriages or improve their relationships. I needed the world to know that though my writing about what it takes to make a great relationship work—that wasn't weird at all. It was all right there, real, and right from the heart. That's how we shared it, and that's how we wrote it. I really hope you will get as much out of it as we put into it.

INTRODUCTION

On a beautiful Saturday afternoon in early fall, I drove my two children to their mother's home where I was to drop them off for the remainder of the weekend. In between the laughter and random questions from the kids, I wondered how I would spend the rest of my weekend without them. My thoughts soon became a full-blown daydream of spending my weekend with an imaginary girlfriend that I was yet to meet. However, my fantasy was quickly interrupted as I pulled into the driveway of my former home.

"Oh, your Aunt Sheryl is here."

They darted out of the car, excited to see her. I grabbed their bags and headed towards the front door to join them. Visiting with Sheryl was enough of an excuse to spend a few extra minutes with the kids.

At that time, I had been divorced for about a year and had already developed a solid and cooperative new relationship with Theresa, my former wife. Surely, we had our share of battling while in the process of divorce, but now things were comfortable and seemed to work for all of us. As I approached the steps, we were greeted by Sheryl, who had responded to the kids' knocking.

"Can you help me with my computer?" she yelled in the friendliest of voices. Sheryl had been a close friend to our family for many years. She was also a recently divorced mother of four. Entering the house, I found that Theresa and Sheryl had been sitting at the kitchen table, working on their computers.

I am certainly not a computer expert, but somehow I had developed the reputation of being able to help fix many of the technology-related problems encountered by family and friends. Actually, my background is in the field of clinical psychology where I had been in private practice for over ten years. As a psychotherapist, I had helped thousands of patients overcome various struggles with depression, anxiety, attention deficits, substance abuse, and relationship issues. While I was well qualified in all of these areas, I became an increasingly sought-after marriage and relationship therapist. Soon into my career, the majority of my patient referrals were for marriage and relationship counseling. Computer technician? Definitely not. Relationship technician? Maybe.

As I fixed her computer, Sheryl began grilling me for the names of single friends that I could introduce her to. "Come on, don't you have any single friends that you can hook me up with?"

While her request seemed reasonable, I could hardly think of any unattached friend that she didn't already know. "Sorry, I'm tapped out . . . Besides, you know all of my friends. I've got nothing for you!" Half-joking, I added, "Why don't you go on Match.com or something?"

Expecting her to laugh, I was surprised when she told me that she had been looking at it and was considering joining. Looking at me with the straightest face, Sheryl challenged me: "I'll do it if you do it!"

And it was at that moment that I half-heartedly agreed to join an online dating website.

Perhaps you're nodding your head in sympathy. Perhaps you've considered joining a dating website yourself and have also checked out Match.com, Plenty of Fish, or eHarmony. Probably, you are single, unattached, and searching for that one magical relationship that will forever change your life. And if you are like me, at least in this story, you probably feel hopeful, but cautiously skeptical.

Fact: There are roughly 58 million American adults who are single. More than 40 million, or nearly 70 percent, of these singles will try online dating this year. So, if you're single and you haven't yet considered utilizing some form of online medium to meet other singles, then you are a member of a shrinking minority. And frankly, you are missing out.

Searching for a romantic partner through Internet dating has truly become an increasingly popular and effective strategy for meeting available singles—and it continues to grow rapidly in terms of clientele usage, business revenue, and even popularity in media and pop culture. Online dating isn't something that only desperate or lonely people do. In fact, it is as legitimate and effective as any of the traditional methods of meeting a mate, not to mention that it's probably more time-efficient. It offers its users some amazing tools that clearly point towards the future of dating, but not everyone is convinced. For a while, even *I* wasn't convinced.

What I didn't know was that I was about to step into a world of endless possibilities that would challenge everything I thought I knew about attraction, dating, attachment, and relationships.

That same afternoon Sheryl and I assembled our online identities by clicking through and affirming traits and characteristics to describe ourselves physically, occupationally, socially, emotionally, and intellectually. Slapping some Facebook photos to our profiles, we created our online identities, paid for a membership, and began to search through the endless pages of available singles in our area.

Wow! To say that I was surprised by the large number of attractive and eligible local women would be an understatement. After thirty minutes of searching through profiles, I drove off with a newfound excitement for dating and meeting new people. I was certainly looking forward to spending some time reviewing and checking out the website later that night. Until…

Before even pulling up in my driveway, I received a text message from my recent ex-girlfriend. Opening the message revealed a screenshot of my Match.com profile and one word: "Nice!"

Despite the fact that we hadn't spoken in over a month, I immediately felt like I was caught red-handed committing some illegal act. Wondering how she found my online profile so quickly, I answered her text with, "Yes, it must be 'nice' for you too! After all, you must have been browsing to find me, right?" She didn't respond.

For the rest of that evening, I was troubled by her comment? Why did she think she could make fun of me for having an online dating profile? These days, it seems that everyone is meeting online. And as I thought about it, I was a bit surprised to recognize that I wasn't the least bit embarrassed by the fact that my ex-girlfriend found my dating profile. At that moment, I also realized that our world has really changed so much in the past ten years. People find one another, become acquainted, and date in ways we couldn't have dreamed of a decade or so ago, and I was *excited*.

My work as a psychologist and relationship therapist has certainly provided me with considerable knowledge on the topics of love, attraction, relationships, and marriage, so when I started dating, I felt confident in my ability to meet and develop relationships with new people. Indeed, I thought it would be a cinch to find love quickly, especially given the amazing tools available to help facilitate my search.

But then the reality of my situation hit me. As exciting as it all seemed, dating in the age of Web 2.0 meant immersing myself in a whole new culture with a whole new set of rules. Rather than being the relationship expert who knew what he was doing, I found myself ill prepared for the online and mobile dating of today's world.

For those of us who have been out of the dating game for some time, online dating, social media dating, or mobile dating can be very, well, intimidating. Once I did venture back into the "scene," though, I quickly realized that learning how to use these tools could open up a world of opportunity at our fingertips and, when used the right way, give us an unprecedented ability to find lifelong love.

While I am still "single" and have yet to meet "The One," I'm certainly not the same single dad with a blasé approach to finding love. Not at all! Putting yourself out there can be an excellent teacher. The excitement, anticipation, butterflies, and attraction you feel when you like someone can be quite a high. But the despondence and despair of not having your feelings reciprocated can cause even the most confident person to question themselves, especially if you haven't dated in a while.

I think it's safe to say that re-entering the dating scene has certainly been an exhilarating experience for both Theresa and me. We've made plenty of mistakes, gone on some crazy dates, and accumulated some hilarious and wonderful stories. But most importantly, we've learned a lot of the new rules for dating in the age of social media and the mobile web. And now we're sharing some of these stories and lessons with you.

If you're having difficulty finding the right person, if you have struggled with past relationships, or if you simply think that dating sucks—this book is for you. We've done our best to not only include tips for handling common dating challenges, but to also explain what makes good, healthy relationships work and thrive. We wrote this book to help you understand those difficult dating situations and the changes necessary to improve your relationships. Through this book, we aim to help you understand why those failed relationships failed and teach you how you can avoid repeating mistakes of the past. Ultimately, we hope that this becomes a tool that will help you prepare for the happy, healthy relationship of your dreams.

We share this book with those of you who believe in fresh starts and second chances. And it is our hope that the lessons we've learned so far from our adventures (and perhaps a few misadventures) will help you in your own quest for lifelong love.

SECTION 1
LET'S START OVER

Wisdom is the gift we receive for having the courage to pursue dreams that no one else can make for us

1
BECOME YOUR OWN CUPID

I'm Single Because—
Settling is something the
pilgrims did in 1620

The desire to find a life partner is a human characteristic and has been a goal of nearly every person since the beginning of recorded history. This desire may partly come from the primal need to reproduce and ensure the continuity of our species, but more than that, who wants to be alone for the rest of their life? Finding someone to spend our life with is so important that marriage has been a fundamental right of passage in nearly every civilization, culture, religion, or way of life. Getting married and having children is something that people have come to expect for themselves. Consequently, finding and forming a romantic partnership is something most people want and expect for their lives.

Children are often asked the question, "What do you want to be when you grow up?" And even the youngest ones will declare: "I want to be a mommy/daddy." Even at a young age, children already consider what it will be like to be married, to an extent that they may even have an idea of what their future partner will look or act like!

People simply thrive when they are coupled, and for good reason. Married people are more likely to enjoy an enduring, supportive, and intimate relationship, and they are less likely to suffer from loneliness. Marriages also provide people with sources of identity and self-esteem as well as an escape from the stresses of one's life. It's no surprise that study after study conducted in the United States and Europe consistently points to the fact that marriage is strongly correlated to individual happiness and health.

So is finding the right partner important? It's probably the most important decision that people ever make. Just as a happy and healthy relationship is related to life satisfaction, an unhappy and dysfunctional relationship can be the source of distress and unhappiness that permeates every aspect of life.

When it comes to finding a life partner in modern times, people often leave things up to fate or destiny, believing that they will cross paths with their soul mate when the time is right. Despite the fact that finding a lifelong love is arguably one of the most important goals for every person ever born, many are comfortable with leaving matters of "love" to chance encounters that are beyond their control. Some might expect that they will be at the same place at the same time and it will naturally happen. My favorite daydream, for instance, is to meet my lifelong love as I'm reaching for a bottle of ketchup in a grocery store. Time suddenly stops, the room starts spinning, and we lock eyes and never look back. Somehow, that sounds magical and divine.

Of course, this can and does happen to many people. Those lucky couples develop a fulfilling relationship that leads to marriage and a long, happy life together. Unfortunately, this is the exception, not the rule.

For those of us who aren't lucky enough to meet our soul mate by chance encounter, finding an appropriate partner can be challenging and frustrating. But not to worry—useful help is often readily available in the form of matchmakers. Parents, friends, and loved ones are often willing to help by playing cupid and taking your love life into their own hands. And it often works. The majority of people actually meet through mutual connections. But what happens to those of us who haven't been so lucky getting introduced through friends or family?

Well, they turn to the "pros."

Historically, the art of matchmaking was handled by pillars in the community who were armed with a broad social network, a belief in their ability to recognize who would make a good couple, and a desire to use their judgment to make those connections. Many of these third-party matchmakers became impressively good at the practice, and they were credited with introducing many loving couples.

Today we have access to more people than ever before. No longer are we limited by physical proximity, the size of our social network, or the availability of singles' activities in our town. Indeed, the Internet opens the doors and levels the playing field, granting us access to the millions of singles all over the world.

Make no mistake about it, though; like achieving any important goal, finding your soul mate is going to require effort, as well as realistic expectations and a well-thought-out plan.

SHORT-TERM GOALS

Finding love when you aren't looking for it is amazing. Equally amazing is finding love when you are searching for it.

When you make the decision to take control of your romantic destiny, you immediately empower yourself to make things happen. As with any major decision, you will begin to qualify your dreams and develop the short- and long-term goals that are necessary to make those dreams a reality.

Let's talk about that.

People are always making resolutions about changing their behavior and accomplishing major goals—quitting smoking, losing weight, finding a significant other—and then fail to fulfill them. But some people do keep their promises to themselves and achieve their goals. They succeed because they set demanding goals that motivate, challenge, and inspire them.

Okay, so you're ready to find your soul mate. Great! But where do you start? It's not an easy thing to do, no matter who you are. There is a lot of discouragement along the way, and it can be difficult to focus on the positive when it seems to take forever to meet your match. Even with a goal such as finding love, though, there are steps you can take that make the process less daunting, less heartrending. You can set short-term goals to help see the progress you're making. We suggest three short-term goals that can help guide you on your way to your long-term one—finding true love.

Here is the route we recommend. Start with defining what a strong relationship looks like to you and how your partner will complement you. Then move into setting your intentions and vision statement. Finally, develop the roadmap you'll take to find that person and take the first step down that path.

One of the hardest things about goal-setting is stepping back and really thinking about what you want. People more often set their goals in the negative ("I don't want to be alone anymore") instead of the positive ("I want to find a love to cherish"). And even when you focus on the positive, it can be difficult to truly define your goal. Take the latter statement, for example: *"I want to find a love to cherish."* It's positive, yes. It's certainly understandable. But it's also poorly defined.

What does love look like to you? We're not just talking appearances, though physical attraction is important. Admittedly, it might not feel appropriate to make a list of the qualities you want in a partner, sort of like making a shopping list or ordering something custom online. This is a person, after all. But this process isn't so much about a cafeteria-style creation of your true love. It's about being honest with yourself about who you are and who will bring out the best in you. There are some things that are incredibly flexible, like looks and career. Then there are other things that are deal-breakers if you don't agree, like having kids. And what about free time? Do you want someone adventurous, or are you more of a Netflix-marathon person? Maybe you want the opposite to bring you out of your shell or bring you back down to Earth. At the end of the day, you need to know yourself and identify what's truly important to you in a relationship, as opposed to what is just "nice to have."

Once you have an idea of the type of relationship you're looking for, it's time to set your intentions and create a relationship vision statement for yourself. I know it sounds a little methodical, but just consider this for a moment. How did the world's leading companies get so successful? And how do they stay successful? That's right, they all have a vision. They have a very clear picture of what they want for their business. It's really that simple.

Now, try to do the same thing for your love life.

The point of a relationship vision statement is to condense your goal into a few words or sentences. It's meant to be short but meaningful. You're not focusing on the "how." Instead, you're focusing on the "what." Really think about what you most want for yourself in terms of having a relationship. After all, it's not always going to be easy and you *will* experience some rough days. Your vision statement has to be something that will always inspire you.

The biggest part of a vision statement is to make yourself and your actions the focal point. It's not about "finding my perfect match," but about being the best you and doing your part. The idea here is to put yourself in the mindset that you deserve to find true love, not because everyone is entitled to it, but because you are going to give yourself the best chance at finding it.

According to the law of attraction, people who put out positive energy to actively find partners are more likely to attract similar people who are also seeking partners. When building a vision statement, you are making a positive intention toward finding love. Your vision statement is essentially your intention put in words. This helps with maintaining the right mindset and getting through the bad dates, the bad break-ups, and ultimately, it will help you find your love.

So now you know what you're looking for, and you're pumped up and ready to find and build that relationship. What's next? How are you going to do it? It's time to write out your roadmap. Of course, there is no easy plan. Unfortunately, it's unpredictable where love will grow or when. But that is also part of its appeal. It's that magical moment you may be hoping for but never really see coming. Roadmaps for big goals, especially love, are meant to be winding and broken and have many different paths. Perhaps the hardest part of seeking a partner is being open to all those different paths.

Of course, we aren't saying you must pursue every single option. You aren't required to go on every blind date, endure rounds of speed-dating, and pay for membership on all the dating websites. But you shouldn't carelessly scoff at them either. Relying on just one source may work, but you may also find yourself with limited options. And options are the point. In the early stages, you want to meet multiple people and put that statement you wrote to the test. It shouldn't be written in stone, because it's very unlikely you'll find a perfect person (though we are sticking to the list of deal-breakers as they apply to you).

With many avenues to walk down, you get to the most nerve-racking part of goal-setting: the part where you actually do. Goal-setting is meaningless if you don't put words into action. So test the waters. Get on the dating sites. Tell people you're looking. You don't need to set up a date every night, or even a date a week. This isn't a sprint, but a marathon. Yes, you may meet your soulmate quickly, and that's great. Don't let it discourage you if that's not the case, though. (Make sure to go back to your vision statement when you feel this way.)

If you take the time to really figure out what you want and put that down on paper, step back, and internalize it, you'll find that this whole process gets easier. When you know who you're looking for, it's not hard to set those intentions. And you'll be more eager, more confident to get started. Embrace the concept of being open and flexible, but when it comes time to commit, be sure that you're staying true to your own heart in the process.

THE JOB SEARCH PLAN

In many ways, finding a life partner is very similar to a job search. Having a career or a job that we are happy with is related to personal happiness and well-being. After all, most of us spend the majority of our waking time with that job. Feeling stuck with a job or career that you dislike can make your life miserable. So, when looking for an ideal job, people recognize the importance of finding the right fit, culture, and values that most closely resemble their own. Makes sense, right?

How does one go about effectively searching for a job? If I were looking for a job, I would utilize every strategy, technique, or tool that I could get my hands on. I would actively search daily without limiting myself to the strategies that I was most accustomed to or comfortable with.

My Job Search Plan would begin with having a good idea of the type of job I was looking for and the places that employ people in that position. I would certainly understand and highlight my strengths on resumes, applications, letters, correspondence, interviews, and follow-ups. I would inquire with all of my family, friends, and former colleagues regarding their knowledge of available jobs. Approaching companies of interest in person, where appropriate, might also be effective. Where cold calling wasn't an option, I would utilize the telephone, e-mail, and snail mail. It might also be helpful to join social media websites like LinkedIn to access a wider network of people in my chosen field. And perhaps most importantly, I would join several job search websites and visit them daily to ensure that I was aware of the available jobs and how to best reach them. Indeed, finding the perfect job would be something that I spent much of my time doing.

Doesn't that sound like an effective plan for finding an ideal job? Guess what? It's also a great plan to use when searching for an amazing partner. Try this: Go back through and reread the last three paragraphs, then replace the word "job/career" with the word "spouse" or "partner."

I've gone through this exercise with hundreds of clients. Many have definitely complained that finding a partner and falling in love isn't something that we can just plan. After all, where's the magic in that? You don't plan magic—you just let it happen.

I strongly disagree.

Sure, "magic" just happens. Many couples will certainly attest to that. But the thing is that once you begin to actively find love, you create a space that will allow that magic to happen. That's you taking matters into your own hands.

2
YOU ARE HERE

Are you ready to date? Remember, two half persons together don't make one full relationship.

Ultimately, the purpose of this book is to teach you the healthy relationship skills that will lead you to find and develop a loving relationship with a compatible partner. This goal, like any challenging or worthwhile goal, is not something that happens automatically. Meeting, getting to know, and falling in love with the right person is a process that requires understanding *where you are now* and the steps you need to take on your road to finding love.

It's very similar to the process a student completes to become a professional. As an example, let me tell you about Taryn, a college freshman attending her first university orientation. Taryn's dream of becoming a teacher began when she was in elementary school, but it was confirmed when she wrote a final paper in a high school career exploration class. She loved the idea of being a teacher and was excited to begin university studies.

During the orientation, Taryn completed her academic placement tests and met with a counselor to create an academic success plan. In addition to helping her create a term-by-term plan, the counselor also talked with Taryn about the challenges and difficulties she could face. By now, Taryn was fully aware that her academic journey would require hard work, dedication, and the ability to overcome any challenging obstacles she might face.

After getting her placement tests scored, Taryn knew exactly what her academic skill level was. And with the help of her counselor, she was informed of the necessary skills she would have to master to become a teacher. Now, Taryn is ready to begin her classes, and she is committed to studying, practicing, and becoming a teacher.

Just like Taryn, you must fully understand your current position before you can take any steps towards achieving any goal. And when it comes to developing an amazing relationship, you must understand your current and past behaviors that led you to this point. Then, you can identify the behaviors that need to be changed as well as new behaviors that need to be practiced.

Examining a failed relationship is painful, but failing to learn from your experiences is tragic!

Our first goal in this book is to show you ways to improve your relationship skills in dating situations that present difficulty for so many people. We will do this by teaching both relationship theory and practical skills to use when faced with common dating challenges. Rather than simply listing specific things to do or not do, we will teach you the knowledge necessary to understand the dynamics of your relationship tendencies. After all, you may not be aware of the elements of your personality that are likely to cause you problems in the future.

Success depends on you. Acquiring knowledge of behaviors that need to be changed is the first step. We will provide you with that knowledge, but making it work for you requires effort and practice. It's the same as when you're acquiring any new skill. You will need to be consciously aware that you are applying it, and you have to keep doing it until the skill is mastered and so well-practiced that it becomes automatic.

I often get questions from my Twitter followers asking about how they should handle a particular relationship problem or concern. Most are a variation of asking my opinion about an incident that occurred or my interpretation of another person's behavior. Regardless of their question or concern, our conversation always begins with me asking them a series of questions about their history of long-term relationships or marriages, their current relationship's history, how frequently they see one another, whether they have children, and other questions. In short, before I can begin to interpret any relationship or situation, I must be informed of the couple's and individual's history. These questions also provoke the person to begin thinking about the problem and engaging in inner dialogue. Obtaining a history also allows me to establish rapport, alleviate any anxiety, provide some reassurance, and facilitate the flow of information necessary for me to effectively develop my opinion and offer suggestions.

This process is essentially the same as what occurs when a patient comes to my office for therapy. The first meeting always begins as a sensitively crafted assessment of their history and the problem(s) that created the need for therapy. Learning the patient's life story begins to paint a picture of the patient's personality characteristics, strengths and weaknesses, interpersonal style, and cultural context from as far back as necessary. Because the conversation is a two-way dialogue, this history-taking session facilitates my understanding of the problems, but also encourages the patient to more completely understand what the issues are. The only way to accurately diagnose any problem and select appropriate treatment is to engage with and fully understand the patient. After all, a mechanic can only fix your car after identifying the malfunction and anything that might have contributed to it, including the possibility of poor driving habits and driver error.

The goal here is to understand how your own personality traits, experiences, and behaviors interacted to result in your unique relationships. Understanding, through exploration and discovery, is the first step before predicting, controlling, or safeguarding against reoccurrences of the emotional pain associated with yet another failed relationship. In other words, before you develop a beautiful and fulfilling partnership, you must first understand how and why you are single.

You're probably wondering if I'm going to ask you to play therapist on yourself? Well, yes, I am. If you were sitting in front of me in my office, I would begin our conversation by asking you to tell me about all of your important relationships beginning with your very first date and ending with your current situation.

Let's try that for a minute. I want you to sit down and really think about your history of dating, and then write out your history as if you were telling it to another person. For each of your relationships, take note of the following:

1. How did you first meet your partner?

2. What are they like? What were your initial impressions when you first met?

3. Describe how the first date was initiated.

4. What was the relationship like in the beginning?

5. Describe the progression and length of the relationship.

6. Describe other important things that were taking place during the relationship, such as where you lived, worked, went to school, and your relationships with friends and family.

7. Describe when you first recognized that things in the relationship were changing.

8. Who initiated the breakup and why? What are the stories that you tell to explain the breakup?

For most people, answering the last question will require the courage and insight to look at their relationships in a new way that was not explored immediately after the breakup. There are a number of reasons that people might avoid immediate relationship analysis. After all, breaking off a serious relationship is usually a very painful experience, especially for a person who doesn't want the relationship to end.

During such times, we are often comforted by friends and family who try to distract us from the painful feelings. Comfort may come in the form of supportive talks where friends and family instinctually blame the initiator for the relationship problems and allow the brokenhearted partner to deflect some blame onto their partner. And when we are certain that the relationship cannot be salvaged, we shift our focus to getting over the breakup with as little suffering as possible, and find distractions while allowing ourselves time to heal.

While this is certainly recommended and effective, by distracting oneself, a person can avoid investigating the dynamics of the failed relationship and the factors that contributed to the breakup. Distracting oneself can also result in losing out on valuable information about how one's own personality and behaviors might have contributed to the relationship ending.

In most cases, one partner wants to dissolve the relationship more than the other and initiates the breakup. Initiators often feel guilty about the breakup and attempt to justify their part in the breakup by focusing on the faults of their partner. This justification allows the initiator to feel more comfortable about themselves and avoid having to dig into and really investigate how and why the relationship went sour. The initiator shifts most of the blame to their partner and misses the opportunity to explore their own contributions.

When evaluation is done after healing, people may find it easier to ask themselves the really tough questions and have the courage to address the behaviors that might have alienated their partner and contributed to the breakup. It is important to also assess why these behaviors occurred. Were they one-time behaviors, situational behaviors, habitual behaviors, or personality characteristics? Understanding the behaviors and personality characteristics that led to conflict in the relationship provides you with the opportunity to learn from the experience. Perhaps you recognize how you could have behaved differently. On the other hand, perhaps the conflict or disagreement resulted from your partner's objection to you standing up for something you believe in. In that case, you might come to the realization that you would do the exact same thing again. This understanding might lead you to the conclusion that you and your partner have very different personalities that were incompatible.

During the writing process, most people will begin to see patterns emerging. You might be surprised by some of the common themes and similarities between the people that you have been involved with. People have often told me that they had no idea that these patterns existed or that they had never noticed that their history had seemingly repeated itself several times. Perhaps you'll notice that the people you've dated have similar looks, personalities, careers, histories, or experiences. Perhaps you will notice that your relationships began in the spring or summer. Or maybe all of your relationships resulted from meeting someone at school or at work. Even still, you might notice that your relationships began during happy or during troubled times in your life.

Engaging in this exercise, many people discover that they are repeatedly attracted to and date people with similar characteristics. It is easy to fall into the belief that this time things will be better because of prior experience. Things that are familiar feel good, easy, and comfortable. Unfortunately, comfort is often mistakenly interpreted as compatible, when in fact some of the comfort is actually based on familiarity rather than on true compatibility. So, when making a fresh start, they engage in the same behaviors they had in the past but expect a different result. We know where that goes . . .

Upon reviewing your history of relationships, you have probably identified certain problems that have happened over and over. From this perspective, it's easy to tell yourself that you won't let those issues repeat again. After all, you are now aware of them and probably know what you don't want. However, there may be some personal issues that you haven't yet fully acknowledged which will have a powerful influence on who you become attracted to, as well as your ability to engage in a healthy relationship. The next section will be devoted to identifying some of the more common personal issues that can lead you to unknowingly engage in unhealthy relationship choices and behaviors.

IS YOUR MOOD KEEPING YOU SINGLE?

A mood disorder such as depression or anxiety can wreak havoc even on an established relationship. While it's true that problems in your primary relationships can be a precursor to a mood disorder, I'm of the belief that for most people, the real problem *is* the depression. I'm willing to stake my reputation on the following statement: A mood disorder may in fact be preventing you from developing an intimate and romantic relationship.

Even in its mildest form, depression can take a toll on your ability to initiate and develop meaningful relationships because of its powerful influence on perception and behavior. Let's take a closer look.

Depression permeates your perception, thinking, and energy in a stealthy manner. It creeps into your mind and slowly envelops your world with a dark cloud of fog that fills your life with doubt and despair. Often, one's mood will change ever so slightly day by day without triggering recognition in the sufferer until depression has taken hold.

When you struggle with depression, engaging in the world around you becomes more difficult. Because it affects your confidence and self-esteem, your ability to accurately perceive interactions with others becomes skewed. You begin to question and criticize yourself and the intentions of others. You also become highly sensitive to criticism from others and tend to take things very personally.

When you struggle with depression, you experience greater levels of guilt and shame and may question your worthiness at work/school or in relationships. Depression saps your energy level as well as your motivation. Depression may make you lose interest in sex and have you feeling disconnected and isolated. Together, these depressive symptoms can make it nearly impossible to initiate new conversations, let alone new relationships.

It's often difficult to accept the possibility that you may be suffering from depression, because it doesn't announce its arrival with acute physical symptoms like fever, acute pain, sneezing, or itchy eyes. Instead, depression creeps in and makes tiny chemical changes in your brain that begin to manifest in changes in thinking, feeling, and doing. Because the change occurs without measurable physical evidence, it's easy for depression sufferers to blame their emotions and thinking on situations that are occurring in their life. For example, it's easy to attribute our lack of energy to something physical. We can blame our lack of motivation at work on a belief that the job is horrible or that we work with annoying people. And, it's easy to blame our partner's lack of sensitivity or understanding for feelings of disconnection and isolation.

People with depression often point to the situations in their life as the source of their illness. In other words, they might say something like, "Of course I'm depressed. My job sucks, I can't pay my bills, my partner is insensitive and dishonest, I'm overweight, and my parents are in ill health."

A Google search on the symptoms of depression will pull up thousands of websites that list the diagnostic criteria and symptoms of depression. Without getting into a Psych 101 discussion on all of the "types" of depression, I do want to alert you to the fact that one form of mild depression known as Dysthymic Disorder is a chronic condition that may fluctuate but impair a person's functioning for several years. Such chronic depression can start to feel like personality characteristics rather than symptoms of a psychological disorder.

My goal in depression here is not to convince you of whether or not you may be suffering from depression, but rather to pique your interest and suggest that you further investigate this possibility if these symptoms remind you of yourself.

In a clinical setting, doctors and psychologists diagnose depression based on what they see in the session as well as from what their patients tell them. This begins with taking note of how the patient presents themselves. More specifically, doctors will carefully study a patient's behavior and disposition, looking at stance, speech, and movement to determine if the person appears to have a "depressed affect." In other words, does a person look sad and depressed? Are their expressions flat and disinterested?

Because my goal is to assist you in finding and developing an amazing relationship, I think it appropriate to also describe how depression might manifest in the scope of a relationship. Below I have listed the typical and official symptoms of depression that you'd find if you conducted a Google search. I have also added some descriptions of symptoms as they might occur in the scope of a relationship.

In addition to their clinical presentation, a diagnosis of depression requires that most of the following symptoms have been present in the past two weeks:

- Persistent sad, "empty," or anxious mood most of the day, nearly every day. *Withdrawn from your partner, uncommunicative, disinterested, or needy of constant affirmation from partner, frequently worried that partner's feelings are changing, fear of abandonment without reason.*

- Loss of interest or ability to experience pleasure from ordinary activities, including sex. *Diminished interest in sex, distrusting of partner's show of affection.*

- Decreased energy, fatigue, feeling "slower." *Lack of motivation or energy to engage in typical relationship activities, such as shopping together or completing projects at home.*

- Changes in sleep patterns. Some experience insomnia; others experience a need for more sleep or oversleeping. Trouble falling asleep at night but significant difficulty waking up and oversleeping, resulting in missing work hours. Additional need to take a nap during the day.

- Changes in eating, with either a significant increase of appetite and weight gain or loss of appetite and accompanying weight loss. Increased appetite for high-sugar/carbohydrate/fat foods, especially at night. Binge eating.

- Irritable mood, easily annoyed by people or circumstances that wouldn't normally have an effect. *Unusually critical or demeaning of partner. Easily finding fault and combative with partner. Sudden and unpredictable outburst of frustration and anger over menial occurrences.*

- Frequent thoughts of death or suicide. *Unusual and sudden references to divorce or ending of relationship.* Note: If you feel you are in crisis, feeling suicidal, or thinking about hurting yourself or others, please call the National Suicide Prevention Lifeline. It is a free, 24-hour hotline at 1-800-273-TALK (8255). Your call will be connected to the crisis center nearest to you. If you are in an emergency, call 911 or go to your nearest emergency room.

- Difficulty with concentration or making decisions. Lowered motivation and difficulty completing routine tasks. Increased use of television, video games, porn sites, or other distractions that consume hours of time that should have been utilized on other responsibilities.

- Feelings of hopelessness and pessimism. *Denial or distrust of partner's love, intentions, and affection.*

- Increase use of alcohol or other recreational drugs, representing a change from prior behavior.

- Mood reactivity or ability to become excited and even happy about upcoming events, vacations, or time spent with specific people. For example, a sufferer might become excited about an upcoming vacation, but towards the end of the vacation, the depressive feelings return, making the last day of vacation unenjoyable. Because a sufferer is able to experience a brighter mood around certain people or happy events, they are more likely to believe their depressed feelings are situational.

- Extreme jealousy, highly sensitive to rejection or criticism, intense reaction or increased sensitivity to rejection.

It's clear that any of the above symptoms can be the source of dissatisfaction and problems in a relationship. In fact, research from the field of relationship psychology repeatedly shows a strong correlation between depression and marital dissatisfaction in both directions. It's easy to understand how an unhappy or toxic relationship can be stressful and disappointing and contribute to the onset of depression. On the other hand, when a person is depressed, they may also find it difficult to be satisfied with their relationship because their perception of their life is negatively distorted—the dark-shaded glasses effect. Because it's often difficult to recognize, depression could be destroying a relationship without either partner being aware of its impact. Nevertheless, by carefully examining one's situation, thoughts, feelings, and behaviors, one can determine whether a mood disorder was a contributing factor to a problematic relationship.

If you can identify with five or more of the symptoms I've listed above, it's likely that depression has hurt your past relationships. But while it takes a lot of courage to look deep within yourself and recognize your own symptoms, only a physician or licensed mental health professional can make a formal diagnosis. The good news is that you can immediately do something about it by contacting your primary care physician and making an appointment to discuss your symptoms.

That brings us to another important and common issue. You might be feeling ashamed to discuss your symptoms with your health care provider or guilty for having these struggles in the first place. Remember, you didn't choose to feel this way, nor did you do anything to cause these struggles. Taking action to contact your doctor is the first step in becoming mentally and emotionally healthy, and it will certainly give you the power to prevent depression from wreaking havoc on your future relationships. So hold your head up high, and be proud of yourself for having the courage to overcome a problem that is too often overlooked.

3
"AM I READY TO DATE, OR NOT?"

STILL HEARTBROKEN?

"The end of your relationship teaches you more about your partner than you could ever learn in the beginning"

There are two strategies for determining if you are ready to date. The first strategy is focused on recovery and healing from the loss of your relationship. In other words, you will first determine if you are *not* ready to date. The second involves assessing your life to determine if you are in the right place emotionally, psychologically, socially, and financially to begin dating. We'll talk about getting relationship-ready in the next chapter. But first, let's talk about heartbreak.

As the song says, breaking up is hard to do. If you've been in a committed relationship in the past, whether it was for months or for years, I am fairly confident that the breaking up part was hard on both of you. All relationships require a shift in both behavior and cognition, and when the relationship ends, whether suddenly or over some time, it can be very unpleasant.

People respond to the dreaded end of a relationship in a number of ways. How they respond depends upon the nature of the relationship itself. For many people, the official ending of the relationship is something that they saw coming for quite a long time, so when it finally happens, they often feel a sense of freedom and relief. On the other hand, some people are blindsided by the ending of a relationship and seem to have the most difficulty trying to cope with and understand what happened.

When a person has difficulty coping with a breakup, they tend to obsess and hold on to that relationship much longer than they should. This will inevitably cause problems with any relationship they enter into afterward. You must be emotionally free from your last relationship before you can begin a new and healthy relationship with someone else.

I can personally recall an experience that I had during the ending of a nine-month relationship. While the relationship was filled with passion and romance, it certainly had an abundance of problems—problems that were unlikely to be resolved given our life circumstances. So, when the relationship ended, I still felt a great deal of love for this person. However, it was quite obvious to me that things were just not going to work out. I do think that love is the strongest force on earth, but sometimes even love isn't enough.

"Am I Ready to Date, or Not?"

I can still remember exactly how I felt the very last time that I saw her, which was when we discussed the ending of our relationship. Although I really wanted to be with her, I knew that ending the relationship was the right thing to do. I will never forget one of the last things that she said to me that day. In the most serious voice, Hailey told me that I would never be able to find anyone as good as her. My immediate thoughts after hearing that must have been quite obvious because I smirked as I thought to myself, "Oh, I will have *no problem* finding someone that is more right for me."

Because I have helped hundreds of people cope with the end of their relationship, I knew exactly what I needed to do to get past this difficult time. I was armed with a great network of social support, a solid interpretation of what I think went wrong in the relationship, and the belief that I was doing the right thing. So, after about a month of "me" time, I became a member of Match.com and began looking for people that I would be interested in dating.

Despite the fact that I should've known better, I started dating too early. I remember perusing the hundreds and hundreds of Match.com profiles and comparing each of those women to my last girlfriend. Without taking the time to adequately review each profile, I quickly dismissed one after another. Meeting these women in person didn't help either. I simply compared each date to Hailey and suffered disappointment after disappointment.

Feeling disappointed isn't the only consequence of premature dating. Going out with people and unfavorably comparing them to your ex can also result in an emotional setback for you. That is, when you start to believe that no one can compare to your ex, your outlook for future relationships begins to look bleak. Believing that your chances of having an amazing relationship are slim will also make your last relationship look better.

The lesson here is a simple one: Dating again before healing from your last relationship results in unfavorably comparing your new dates to your ex. Disappointing experiences may cause you to doubt the possibility of finding viable and better alternatives and keep you stuck on your last relationship.

"AM I STILL HUNG UP ON MY EX?"

A broken relationship is like a shattered vase; it may be better to leave it broken than to hurt yourself again trying to fix it.

RUMINATE MUCH?

There are some very obvious and many not-so-obvious clues that can help you determine if you're ready for a new relationship. The first and most important clue is the amount of time you spend thinking about your ex every day. Psychologists define ruminating as passively and repeatedly focusing and thinking about a situation, its causes, and its consequences. If you find yourself frequently caught in a loop, replaying memories and past conversations, or if you are fantasizing about what you might say to your ex in a conversation, then you are ruminating about your ex. If you catch yourself doing this frequently, you probably haven't recovered enough to begin thinking about dating.

MAKING COMPARISONS

Just as I did with Hailey, if you find yourself unfavorably comparing potential dates to your ex, you are probably not ready to begin dating. If your last relationship was unhealthy and problematic, you might find yourself making comparisons and even idealizing a potential date because they seem to have the opposite qualities of your ex. While tempting, the fact that you are even making such comparisons is a sign that it's still too soon.

ANGER OR GUILT

As we will discuss later, anger is the second stage after denial in the grief and loss process. We begin to feel anger or guilt after our denial of the loss starts to wane and the pain of the breakup reemerges. For most people, anger is directed at their ex-partner or at the circumstances that led to the breakup. For example, if your relationship ended because of infidelity, you might be angry with your ex-partner for cheating and angry with the other person for being a "home-wrecker." On the other hand, if you were in a relationship with a person who was emotionally abusive, you might be angry with yourself for getting involved with such a person.

On the other side of anger, many newly single people experience a tremendous amount of guilt and blame for the relationship ending. This is particularly true for those partners who are guilty of engaging in outside affairs, cheating, or emotional or physical abuse. Knowing that they are mostly at fault for the relationship ending, they may desperately attempt to undo the damage or "make up" for what they have done and recover the relationship.

When their efforts are rebuffed, they experience the most trouble recovering from the loss.

If you are feeling a significant amount of guilt or anger towards your ex, you are certainly not ready to begin a new relationship.

COMMUNICATING AND NEGOTIATING

The ending of a relationship means that two people who have shared so much together must now untangle and separate so many parts of their lives. As you might expect, it's nearly impossible for this to happen without some type of a transitional period. Despite the fact that you have mutually agreed to end the relationship, there is usually property to be exchanged and moved, as well as other loose ends that might need to be tied up. These issues might require you to continue communicating with your ex-partner as you accomplish the tasks of separating. Many people find that these communications sometimes include negotiation and reevaluation to confirm that this is indeed what you both want. Frequently, during this period couples will make another attempt at making a relationship work. If you are at a stage where you would still consider getting back with your ex-partner, then you are probably not ready for a new relationship.

HUNTING AND HAUNTING

Before you text or call your ex, stop and ask yourself one question...
What will happen if I don't?

When a former couple gets past the negotiation stage and all communication has stopped, many newly single people find that they are engaging in what I call "hunting and haunting." Hunting involves going to places where there is a high probability of running into an ex-partner. This might include frequenting restaurants, bars, and nightclubs that otherwise haven't been part of your stomping grounds. In doing so, the Hunter fantasizes that their ex-partner will suddenly and dramatically have their feelings rekindled after a "coincidental" meeting. Unfortunately, the "coincidental" meeting is awkward at best, and it might even look desperate. Haunting refers to behaviors like driving by the ex-partner's home or place of business at different times in hopes that nothing in their life has changed dramatically. Haunting might also include stalking your ex-partner on Facebook and other social media sites.

Hunting and haunting is detrimental to your recovery for a number of reasons. First, it requires you to spend considerable time and energy thinking about your ex-partner and what they might be doing. If you were to find evidence that your ex-partner might be moving on, it's likely that you will make an unfavorable comparison to your life and start ruminating about your loss. If the information that you learn is incomplete, then you will be tempted to investigate and test your hypothesis. Again, this will result in spending additional time focusing on your ex, instead of focusing on things you could be doing to speed up your recovery. Those of you who have experienced this know that it can certainly result in a setback of your recovery.

I have always been an advocate of the "Out of Sight, Out of Mind" approach to a relationship's end. I believe it is best to stop all communication (if possible) and disconnect ("unfriend") yourselves on social media. I even recommend that you "hide" mutual friends to minimize the possibility of seeing your ex-partner in a loving embrace with another person on Facebook.

If you are still hunting for and haunting your ex-partner, you definitely shouldn't be seeking a new relationship.

> *If it's over, accept it! Acceptance allows the healing to begin and facilitates a quicker recovery from sadness.*

DESPERATION

Some say, "If you want to get over someone, you've got to get under someone new." I'd say that is a dangerous idea. Sure, rebounding can help take the focus off of your ex-partner and provide a needed boost in self-esteem. But accepting an undesirable but available new partner could be even worse. Besides, you would just be kicking your can of problems down the road. If you are feeling desperate and you're uncomfortable with being single, then you are certainly not ready to begin a relationship with anyone but yourself. As we will discuss in Chapter 3, you must be comfortably and happily single before you are ready to begin any new relationship.

NOBODY'S PERFECT
"ARE MY EXPECTATIONS TOO HIGH?"

Most single people have a good idea of what their "type" is, and they know what qualities they desire in a future partner. Usually, their expectations are reasonable and understandable, but there are always some who have a laundry list of expectations that are nearly impossible for any person to meet. Over the years, I have worked with many people who have come to me with such lists. Many of these unrealistic lists include height and weight requirements, eye color requirements, educational requirements, narrow age ranges, and income requirements. Others include idealistic character traits like honesty, empathy, thoughtfulness, selflessness, kindness, compassion, adventurousness, creativity, generosity, ambitiousness, confidence . . . The list goes on and on. While this might sound wonderful to them, you have to wonder, is it reasonable?

Having some of these expectations is customary and expected, but we cannot hold on to unrealistic expectations that are nearly impossible to meet. We cannot expect our future partner to be "perfect" and possess all of these unreasonable qualities. Again, our partners are not perfect, and neither are we. After all, perfect doesn't exist.

Meanwhile, there are also people who have a list of their "deal-breakers." Deal-breakers are specific, individual issues or characteristics of a potential partner that one cannot overlook despite the other redeeming qualities the individual may possess. The deal-breaker is the primary reason for not pursuing or furthering the relationship. For example, "The cat was my deal-breaker. I'm highly allergic to cats, and she was unable to give hers up."

Seinfeld fans will remember that Jerry often broke up with so many amazing women for some ridiculous minor flaw. He dumped a woman for having "man hands" and another for having a "terrible laugh." Jerry stopped dating a woman because he thought she had fake breasts, and he ended another relationship because she was "a sentence-finisher." Obviously, Jerry's reasons were silly and outlandish, but they aren't terribly different from some of the superficial deal-breaker rules that some single people adhere to. Having too many of these deal-breakers will significantly narrow your pool of potential dates.

Creating a list of superficial deal-breakers and sticking to them is limiting. Saying that you're only interested in dating fashion-forward, blue-eyed, Jewish physicians between the ages of thirty to thirty-one and who also live within five miles will make for a long single life. Passing on a Jewish physician because he dressed poorly and was thirty-three years old is superficial. But if religion is important to you, then you might have a problem with a man who meets all the other characteristics but is Catholic.

It's a good idea to come up with a list of your core values, and then create a list of deal-breakers based on those. The deal-breakers list should include important characteristics of one's personality, history, and core values that would make a relationship with you nearly impossible. These are expectations that you hold near and dear and should not be negotiable.

One of the most common deal-breakers or expectations that I've come across is concerned with one's desire and willingness to have children. A single woman who has always dreamed of being a mother should not pursue a relationship with a man who states that he "never wants children." Being a parent is an incredibly important life goal for so many people. It's certainly not one that should be compromised on.

Some say that there is a fine line between settling just to be with someone and being so picky that we remain alone forever. Here's a list of a few signs that your expectations might be too high.

SUPERFICIAL DEAL-BREAKERS

If your list of partner qualities are superficial and include mostly physical characteristics, such as eye color and hair color, you are probably focusing on things that are not important. Again, you should be focusing on core value characteristics and personality characteristics above all.

CLONE-SEEKING

Expecting your partner to be exactly like you is unrealistic. While having similar values, cultural background, and educational background may be important, don't expect to find a person who is exactly the same age, has the same thoughts, ideas, or political views as you do, and also likes the same food, music, movies, sports, and TV programs.

CONSTANT REJECTION

Let's face it—sometimes people need a reality check. A fifty-year-old man who frequents college bars and hits on nineteen- and twenty-year-old women is probably going to get turned down quite a bit. Obviously, his expectations are out of line, and he's probably delusional too. If you find yourself getting rejected a lot, perhaps you should reevaluate your expectations and approach people who are in your generation.

On the other hand, if you are realistic in your expectations yet still finding yourself being rejected most of the time, it may be time to explore and evaluate the ways you are engaging with the people you are attracted to. Was there something that you did that might have put off the other person? Perhaps a joke you made was misconstrued or misinterpreted. Or, were you drinking or smoking cigarettes while with that person? Something as simple as a difference in lifestyle could explain everything. So, conduct an in-depth probe of your personality, attitude, and behavior. There may be ways that you need to change. These are just a few reasons; there could be several more. Wouldn't it be ironic, if after all your detailed reasoning, you discover that the cause for rejection is merely a different sexual orientation from yours?

"BUT WHAT IF I GET REJECTED?"

Even a severe toothache may seem mild in comparison to the emotional agony you experience when a person you really like rejects you. Sure, we know that one person's opinion of you should not matter so much, and we will all experience rejection sometime. Nevertheless, it stings until you get over it.

Let's talk about rejection and some strategies you can use to cope with those feelings and push forward.

When rejected by a romantic interest, we automatically begin looking for the reason behind it. Psychologists call these thoughts and perceptions our "attributions," or our internal explanations we use to try to understand others. Attributions and attributional style have important implications for the self and the way we feel. Research suggests that attributions influence a person's mood, behavior, attitudes, thoughts, motivation, self-concept, reactions to others, personal growth, and expectations of future events, in both positive or negative ways. In other words, the meanings we associate to the events in our lives have everything to do with the way we feel.

When we get rejected, our attributions can take many directions and go haywire. Often, we assume that the rejection was due to some personal shortcoming. When this happens, we are going to struggle to overcome feelings of negativity and dejection. But do we really know the reasons that another person wasn't interested?

The next time you feel rejected by someone, take out a sheet of paper and divide it into two columns. Title the first column "Reasons that have to do with me," and title the second column "Reasons that have nothing to do with me." Then begin listing all of the possible reasons for the rejection. It is probably easiest to begin listing reasons associated with you, so go ahead and get those down first. Then, you have to think of two possible reasons that have nothing to do with you, for every reason you listed in the left column.

For most, an honest self-evaluation will be very revealing, but some people will struggle with recognizing how their behavior sabotages the possibility of success with potential dates. If that is your experience, enlisting the help of a professional dating coach or relationship therapist might be the most effective way to turn your dating dilemmas into dating delight! We discuss getting additional help in Chapter 3.

RELATIONSHIP FANTASIES

Do you maintain fairy-tale love fantasies of how a relationship begins and progresses? Some people believe that they are going to meet that "one soul mate" who will magically sweep them off their feet, deliver "true love's kiss," and awaken them to glories they never knew existed. They believe that they should be able to recognize their soul mate instantly. When they meet a person who fails to deliver that instantaneous magic, they quickly dismiss them as "Not The One." And because they are quick to judge, they often reject people who may have otherwise made amazing partners.

We all want to be involved in an extraordinary relationship, one with all the fire and magic that we see in the movies. But are we really ready for that relationship? We're not perfect, but we need to feel good about ourselves. We have to be happy living in our own skin before we can make any relationship work. Most importantly, we can't let our fear of rejection keep us from taking that next step. As the old saying goes, it's better to have loved and lost than never to have loved at all. So let's take an honestly brutal inventory of ourselves and see if we need to improve in any area. Then we need to take action.

What do you think when you look in the mirror? Are you comfortable with what you see? Are you currently presenting the best version of you possible? We'll become less afraid of rejection as we begin to feel better about ourselves. So, if you feel afraid of rejection, then you have some work to do on yourself. You need to find out why you feel this way, because unless you get a sense of self-esteem, you will find yourself insecure and always afraid of being rejected.

So the next question is this: What defines us? We have to realize that our many life experiences remind us of our imperfections, so we need to learn to embrace and accept them. They are a part of us. Of course, the ones that we can change, we should—waking up crabby, continually judging others, being mean to the neighbor's cat. But those we can't change—the mole on our face, the fact that we are shorter than average—we have to learn to appreciate, because we own them. And beyond our physical characteristics, what else do we own? What are we passionate about? What makes us unique? All of these things are what truly complete us, further identify us, and make us the individual we are. It is not always easy to accept your imperfections or appreciate what makes you different, but once you do, you'll begin to find peace within and admiration from others.

Where is the fear of rejection coming from? Is it that last relationship when your significant other made you feel incompetent, inferior, and insecure? They took you to a place where you lost yourself and had no inner voice, like a child. But this is not a place of no return. You have the ability to recognize that, with self-evaluation and honest work, you can turn this around.

TO DATE OR NOT TO DATE; FOR DIVORCED PARENTS, THE STRUGGLE IS REAL!

At a family dinner the other night, my cousin recounted a joke she played on me. Grace tried to embarrass me while I was pumping gas last week. I chatted with a woman on a different pump as she wiped the overflow of gasoline that spilled on her car. Grace lowered her window and called out "Honey! Are you almost finished? We don't want to be late sweetheart!"

My family is well aware of my history of pranking Grace. So, her story was well received and had everyone laughing. That is, everyone except for my eleven-year-old daughter, Gianna.

Instead, Gianna jumped up, gave Grace a high-five and thanked her for ending my conversation. She continued to ask Grace to describe the woman I talked with and then thanked her again. I was surprised by Gianna's response because her mother and I have been divorced for over four years. I guess she's still not comfortable with the thought of her dad dating again. That's understandable; adjusting to the fact that your parents are dating is difficult for most children. And, it can be very intimidating for divorced parents as well. In addition to the usual challenges that dating presents, divorced parents face three important questions:

1. Are you ready to begin dating?

2. Are your children ready for you to begin dating?

3. Are you ready to introduce your children to a new partner?

This section addresses these questions and offers tips to help you (and your children) transition through a difficult time. I expect some people will find it difficult to agree with my suggestions. After all, "Take things slowly with Mr. or Miss. Wonderful" is not advice that is easy to hear. That said, here are my general suggestions for dating after divorce.

ARE YOU READY TO BEGIN DATING?

A divorce is probably one of the most painful and difficult experiences you will ever have. It can turn your life upside-down. Divorce involves separating your identity from your 'other half' and starting life over again as a single person. And when you have children together, the difficulty is compounded by helping your children cope with their new reality. Healing takes time and a conscious effort.

I'm often asked to how long it takes to recover emotionally. While every situation is different, most people start to enjoy life again within six to twelve months after the divorce is final. Of course, that depends on the length of their marriage. Add one month to those numbers for every year of marriage after the first.

For many newly divorced parents, dating again is the last thing on their mind. Others believe that dating can help take the focus off their ex-partner and provide a needed boost in self-esteem. Either way, professionals suggest that divorced parents with school age children wait at least a year before they begin dating again. While dating again can be exciting and offer temporary distraction from your grief, beginning too soon may set you (and your children) up for more disappointment. What's important is that you recognize when it's too early to think about someone new.

ARE YOUR CHILDREN READY?

Some parents are relieved to sign the divorce papers and feel like they can finally move on with life. But their children face a different reality. Legal finalization is often the beginning of the difficult family transitions they must handle. As parents move out of the marriage home and into separate residences, children face changes in daily routines as well as changes in supervision. Some will have to move from their primary home into a new neighborhood with different schools and peer groups. As a parent, you might experience relief and newfound freedom, but your children are just beginning to feel overwhelmed.

When you've decided that you're emotionally ready to begin dating again, you'll need to consider how difficult it will be for your children. If they're having difficulty adjusting to their new life, adding another change will certainly complicate things.

Children find parental dating stressful for several reasons. Many will worry about having to share you with someone else. Others may be threatened and fear that if you fall in love, you'll have less love for them. And for some children, the realization that their parents are dating again shatters any remaining hopes for their parents to reunite.

Your children are probably going to be anxious when you begin dating. That's why it's important to begin talking with your children and exploring their feelings before you sign up for your favorite online dating site. Invite them to talk about their fears, empathize with them, and validate their feelings. Reassurance that your love and care for them will not change goes a long way. So give them concrete examples of important family experiences that will always stay the same.

SHOULD YOU INTRODUCE YOUR NEW PARTNER TO YOUR CHILDREN?

Most professionals recommend waiting until a relationship is serious before introducing your children. In my opinion, serious means you've been exclusively dating for at least six months and both see a future together. If you cannot see yourself with this person long term, it's best skip that introduction.

When you're ready, talk with your children about introducing them to your new partner. Plan a casual, but fun activity that your children will enjoy, tell them what to expect, and explain what you expect from them. Don't be surprised if your children don't take an immediate liking to your new friend. Take it slow and give your children the time they need to adjust. If you push the relationship on them too quickly, your plan will likely backfire and cause more problems.

The good news is your children want you to be happy. Address their fears and give them some time. Then they will be happy about your new relationship too!

4
GETTING RELATIONSHIP-READY

With self-love, red flags become rest stops. Time for reflection, reevaluation and reconsidering.

LOVING YOURSELF

"WHAT IS 'SELF-LOVE,' EXACTLY?"

What does it mean to love yourself? The question seems simple enough, but when asked what it means to "love yourself," many stumble to find a good definition. Yet somehow when we speak of self-love, most people have some concept of what we're talking about. And when it comes to successful relationships, it's a popularly held belief that self-love is a necessary precursor for a loving partnership.

Defining self-love may be difficult in itself, but understanding how it contributes to successful relationships is even more elusive. Nevertheless, interest in the concept of self-love is widespread and has expanded rapidly within the past twenty years.

One only has to conduct an Internet search to reveal a large selection of authors, websites, and books promoting the importance of achieving self-love. But what exactly is self-love, and why is it so important for intimate relationships?

If you look in the dictionary, you'll see a definition of self-love that doesn't sound very healthy. For example, the Merriam-Webster dictionary defines self-love as a) conceit, and b) regard for one's own happiness or advantage. That definition sounds way too much like narcissism and selfishness. Dictionary.com's definition doesn't sound very positive, either. They define self-love as an instinct by which one's actions are directed to the promotion of one's own welfare or well-being, conceit, vanity, and narcissism. Certainly, those traits can't be related to successful relationships!

Thankfully, psychologists and philosophers explain self-love as a very positive concept, which incorporates and combines several positive, self-enhancing qualities of thinking, feeling, and acting towards yourself. For example, psychologist Erich Fromm proposed that loving oneself means caring about oneself, taking responsibility for oneself, respecting oneself, and realistically and honestly knowing oneself. He further contrasts self-love with selfishness in *The Art of Loving:* "Selfishness and self-love, far from being identical, are actually opposites." p.47

Fromm's description of self-love is a good start, but a more operational definition was given by psychologist Dr. David Patrick in his doctoral dissertation of 1982. Dr. Patrick proposed a model of self-love that includes positive experiences expressed through 1) thoughts, 2) feelings, and 3) behaviors towards ourselves.

In other words, self-love is characterized by high, positive, self-enhancing quality of thinking, feeling, and acting towards yourself. These three component processes are further divided into the six component processes that together make up the experience of self-love: self-attachment, self-affection, positive self-regard, self-worth, self-knowing, and self-caring. Let's take a closer look at what these components mean and how they are expressed.

SELF-ATTACHMENT

Self-attachment is the feeling of ownership, desire, or belongingness to one's self. It is taking pride in who you are. High levels of self-attachment means that you want to be just the person you are. Self-attachment gives you the drive to be responsive to your own ends for self-maintenance and growth. A person with a high level of self-attachment tries to be aware of what is best for themselves. High self-attachment means that you try to act in ways that make your life enjoyable and satisfying.

SELF-AFFECTION

Self-affection is the sensation of liking and feeling satisfied and excited about one's experiences. It's being able to feel enjoyment in activities that you engage in. Self-affection is feeling warm inside when you think of yourself, feeling at peace with yourself, and being able to enjoy your own company.

POSITIVE SELF-REGARD

Positive self-regard is an enduring attitude of valuing the self. This includes self-esteem, self-respect, and self-acceptance. A person with high positive self-regard recognizes their life as important and valuable despite their successes, failures, or status. People with high positive self-regard accept their limitations and inadequacies fairly well and know that they are a good person despite their faults.

SELF-WORTH

Self-worth is an individual's belief that they are a valuable person and that life is a valued possession. This also includes self-confidence, or the belief in one's ability to master themselves and their life. Self-worth also includes the belief that one is able to love themselves and that they are able to respond to their needs in an accurate and productive manner.

SELF-KNOWING

Self-knowing involves the process of reflective thinking in reviewing of one's thoughts, feelings, and behaviors. It involves the ability to see oneself from the outside and is the basis for being able to respond accurately to one's needs. Self-knowing is being able to listen to, know, and understand your own feelings as the basis for taking action that is best suited for yourself.

SELF-CARING

Self-care includes the behaviors we engage in that are aimed at maintaining the health and welfare of the self. Maintenance involves responding to one's needs and taking precautions to ensure one's psychological and physical health. This might include avoiding undue stress and destructive habits and engaging in healthy eating, exercising, and living. Self-caring also involves responding appropriately to reduce pain and stress when it does occur. Finally, self-care also includes behaviors intended for enhancing and growing. Self-enhancement refers to behaviors and expanding one's talents, education, or relationships with others.

"HOW CAN I PRACTICE SELF-LOVE?"

Up to this point, we've discussed what self-love isn't and what it is. These definitions are helpful, but a few practical explanations of practicing self-love in the real world will help to solidify the concept for you. Let's begin by examining the way a self-loving person thinks about and treats themselves. Trying to understand the concept of relating to yourself can seem strange, and you might even feel like you are getting in your own way. So, to simplify things, I want you to think about what a healthy relationship between a parent and a child is like. I also want you to picture yourself in the role of the parent and try to imagine yourself experiencing the feelings, thoughts, and actions that I describe in these examples. Focus on how a loving parent would feel as they relate to their child.

A good parent takes pride in their child and gives them a sense of identity and belonging to the family. A good parent is responsive to their child's needs for safety, health, and happiness. Good parents are aware of what is best for their child and try to act in ways that make the child's life more joyful and satisfying. A person who is able to relate to themselves in this manner is practicing a high level of **self-attachment.**

A great parent certainly feels love for their child and feels enjoyment when engaging with or playing with them. A great parent enjoys the company of their children. A loving parent feels warm inside when they think of their child and feels at peace when they know that their child is happy. When you are able to relate to yourself in this manner, then you are practicing **self-affection**. Can you see where I'm going with this?

A good parent is supportive of their child and holds high—but realistic—expectations of them. After all, a good parent wants their child to excel and succeed. When your child makes mistakes or gets into trouble, you don't devalue them or love them any less. Instead, a good parent helps their child to understand and learn from their mistakes through nurturing and support. Being able to treat yourself in these ways is practicing **positive self-regard**.

A loving parent knows that their child is valuable as a person and is confident in their belief that their child can make a great life for themselves. A loving parent recognizes and appreciates the love shared between parent and child and feels confident in their ability to anticipate and respond to the child's needs. Relating to yourself in this way is engaging in the practice of **self-worth.**

Great parents listen to their children's thoughts and seek to know and understand their feelings. These parents use this knowledge and understanding to take action with their child's best interest at heart. Being able to reflect upon, learn, and understand your thoughts, feelings, and behaviors in this manner is the practice of **self-knowing**.

Lastly, a loving parent is concerned for and dedicated to maintaining the health, welfare, and safety of their child. These parents educate their children on healthy eating and the value of exercise and teach them to live a healthy lifestyle. They do their best to protect their child physically and psychologically and seek immediate care when the child is ill or in pain. When a person treats themselves in this manner, they are practicing **self-caring.**

"HOW IS SELF-LOVE CONNECTED TO RELATIONSHIPS?"

At this point, you might agree that self-love is a practice that is psychologically healthy and related to confidence, high self-esteem, and taking good care of yourself physically. Self-love is also thought to be a precursor to a healthy and happy love life. But how does "self-love" contribute to finding the right partner and developing a great relationship? Let's explore these questions by looking at some real life examples.

"STAYING IN AN UNHEALTHY RELATIONSHIP TOO LONG WILL MAKE A ONCE HEALTHY PARTNER UNHEALTHY!"

Amber is a 30 year old nurse who has been single for about 18 months. Prior to that, she was engaged and living with Ryan, a young doctor she met at work. The couple had been dating for about a year when Ryan asked Amber to move into his apartment. Shortly thereafter, Ryan proposed to Amber and the couple planned to marry after he completed his residency.

As a resident, Ryan worked long hours and struggled to keep up with the demands of his medical program. He was constantly over-stressed and began drinking nightly, claiming that he needed something to help him sleep. At first he would only drink one glass of wine at bedtime, but before long, he was drinking more than one bottle per day. Ryan also became increasingly verbally abusive and angry and even pushed Amber causing her to trip and sprain her wrist. After the second time he assaulted her, Amber broke-off the engagement and moved out of the apartment. She also quit her job at the hospital to avoid having to interact with Ryan on a daily basis.

Over the next several months, Amber spent a significant amount of time thinking about her relationship and tried to understand how it got so bad. She was committed to understanding and learning from it and promised herself that she wouldn't allow herself to remain in any toxic relationship in the future. She began reading books about abusive relationships and focused on growing from her experience. She was also hired at another hospital and found herself feeling happier and more confident.

Amber had many opportunities to date, but she wanted to wait until she was completely over Ryan. She remained single for about 10 months before feeling that she was ready to start dating again. Because her sister met her husband online, Amber thought it might also be a good place for her to look. So, she logged on to Match.com and created her first online dating profile.

Within hours dozens of email messages from attractive, successful, and eligible men filled her mailbox. She communicated with many of them through a series of messages and even exchanged phone numbers with the three men that she found most interesting. Over the next few weeks, she met and went on a date with each of them. Her first two dates seemed nice enough, but neither would come close to the attraction and chemistry Amber felt for Jacob.

Jacob was a 34 year old banker who was very handsome, successful and athletic. On their first date, the conversation was natural and fluid and Jacob had Amber laughing the whole night. They held hands as they walked to her car where the couple kissed passionately before saying goodbye. As she drove away, Amber could hardly contain her excitement and immediately called her best friend to tell her about her date.

The next day, Amber thought about Jacob all day. She joked with her girlfriend saying, "I thought he was out of my league" and blushed when she talked about the chemistry she felt. Their second date went even better than the first and resulted in the couple spending the night together at Jacob's house. From that point forward, they decided to date each other exclusively and spent every night together.

The couples' affection for one another grew quickly and Amber was proud to tell her friends and family that they never argued or fought. To an outsider, their young relationship might have appeared to be perfect. Indeed, the couple hardly disagreed with one another, but this was due to the fact that Amber went along and agreed with everything Jacob wanted. Instead of speaking up and expressing herself when she disagreed, Amber preferred to agree and avoid having a debate. The same was true with regard to friends and activities. The couple spent most of their time together engaging in Jacob's hobbies with his friends and family.

Amber no longer called her girlfriends to make plans, nor did she insist that they do things with her family.

Amber was also very pampering of her man and "took good care of him". She sent him text messages throughout the day to remind him of her affection and love. She surprised him with little gifts and cards, cleaned his apartment, and did his laundry. Trying to anticipate his needs, Amber frequently did thoughtful favors for Jacob without him asking. Jacob even told Amber that no one had ever been so good to him, yet he hardly returned her favors. She told herself that she was being selfless, loving, and ideal, so she continued to put herself last.

Amber secretly hoped that Jacob would fall deeply in love with her and begin to inquire about and fulfill her needs without her ever having to ask for them. It seems that Amber subscribed to the belief that people will like you more if you always agree to their ideas or activity choices. She also believes that her thoughtfulness, agreeableness and love should get the same in return. Unfortunately, Amber's turn never came and the relationship remained lopsided.

The couple had been dating for about one year when Amber began feeling disappointed with her relationship. Because she invested so much more time and energy into the relationship, she felt that she loved Jacob more than he loved her. Her agreeableness started to wear thin and she started to resent Jacob, feeling neglected or taken advantage of. Her resentment lead to repeated arguments and fighting and Amber became more insecure with the relationship. Jacob also sensed her insecurity and felt that

Amber had grown more needy. Before long, Jacob began feeling like something was missing and decided he needed to end the relationship because his feelings for Amber had changed.

Most of us can relate to this scenario in some way. In fact, relationships like Amber's are very common. Perhaps we have friends who have engaged in similar behaviors and have had similar results. Or, maybe Amber's relationship is similar to one that you've personally experienced. Either way, there are several possible explanations for Amber's pattern of behavior.

Clearly, Amber began the relationship with the best of intentions. She wanted to be the best girlfriend possible but may have felt that Jacob was "Out of her league". This underlying insecurity motivated the way she interacted with Jacob. Fearing that she wasn't good enough, Amber created the façade of the perfect girlfriend who loved everything that Jacob loved, including his friends, family, and hobbies. In essence, Amber had to make herself the woman she thought would be most impressive to Jacob and win his heart. This required Amber to constantly self-observe and be on her "best behavior" for prolonged periods of time. Engaging in such behavior is incredibly stressful and eventually causes feelings of resentment, depression, or anger towards the partner and oneself.

Amber overestimated her ability to maintain her façade. Within months of meeting Jacob, she tired of being the "perfect girlfriend" and "enjoying" what Jacob had come to expect. Maybe Amber hoped to hide her true self long enough for Jacob to fall so deeply in love with her outward façade that he wouldn't be able to leave when the real Amber showed up.

Putting a partner's needs first can be a beautiful gift; but only between partners who can share equally in the GIVING and RECEIVING.

"SELF – LOVE: FAKE IT UNTIL YOU MAKE IT"

In the example above, Amber was definitely not practicing self-love. But, where intimate relationships are concerned, practicing self-love can be tricky and difficult. Often, we get in our own way because our brains manipulate our thoughts and actions in order to protect us from recognizing unacceptable truths about ourselves. Amber feared that if she engaged in the behaviors representative of her true feelings, Jacob might not like her as much. So, rather than acknowledge her feelings of inferiority, Amber became an actress and played the part of Jacob's "perfect girlfriend".

When a person engages in self-deception like Amber did, they create an experience and belief about themselves that is far from objective or accurate. Then they use self-justification to explain, defend, and glorify their thoughts and behaviors. And by blinding themselves to their true motivations and feelings, they unwittingly sabotage their own efforts for happy and satisfying relationships.

So, Amber created this simulated personality and buried herself in her self-deception. Although Amber was unable to see her destructive behaviors, her closest friends and family recognized it from the beginning and tried to address their concerns. Unfortunately, her friends' attempts to communicate these observations resulted in Amber avoiding them and further isolating herself in Jacob's world.

"BECOME YOUR OWN BEST FRIEND"

Sometimes you just have to forget what you feel, and remember what you deserve.

As we discussed above, practicing self-love in the context of a new intimate relationship is often easier said than done. When we want another person, we often do things that we think will win their affection. And in doing so, many people engage in behaviors that are anything but self-loving. The good news is that if we commit to becoming our own best friend, we can learn to practice self-love while developing amazingly fulfilling and loving relationships. But, it all starts with learning to be your own best friend.

"PRACTICE, PRACTICE, PRACTICE"

People don't become best friends overnight. Instead, they spend alone time together and cultivate their relationship through honest communication and sharing. The same is true for becoming your own best friend. You must spend quiet time getting to know yourself through self-reflection and introspection. Make it a priority every day to spend 10-15 minutes in solitude where you simply think about yourself and your life. Get yourself a notebook and begin writing your thoughts and journaling during this time.

Writing will help you stay on task and focused only on yourself. Write about what you really like and dislike, write about what drives and motivates you, and write about your goals and dreams for the future. Write as if you are speaking to your future self and express your thoughts, beliefs and feelings about the important things in your life.

Best friends also plan and share enjoyable activities with one another. Becoming your own best friend will require you to plan and enjoy activities by yourself. As you journal, develop a list of activities that you can enjoy doing alone. These solo activities can be hobbies such as exercising, reading, writing, listening to great music, meditating, or engaging in the fine arts. Practicing these hobbies will help you to appreciate your own company, deepen your understanding of yourself, and help you to cultivate self-love.

Best friends really listen to one another and offer the safety of trust as they share their true thoughts and feelings. They support one another with acceptance and encouragement, but sometimes have to practice tough love when we need it. It's important that one can also engage in this type of acceptance and encouragement for ourselves. Being able to comfort and encourage yourself through difficult times will require regular practice. Practice talking to yourself as you would talk to a best friend. So, when you are struggling or upset about a situation, think about the words you would say to your best friend and then say them to yourself. Allow yourself to feel supported and accepted.

"THE BEST FRIEND TEST"

New relationships can be exhilarating, thrilling and super exciting when things are going well. But they can also be stressful and unsettling when things just aren't right. Rather than walk away from something that will never work, many are willing to go to great lengths trying to make things right. In an effort to change their new partner's behavior or win their affection, they compromise their values and beliefs and try to become what they think their partner wants. Of course, compromising your values and beliefs is far from healthy or self-loving.

When entering a new relationship, practicing self-love may require you to look at your life through the lens of being your own best friend. Doing so means that you take time to honestly reflect on your situation as you would if your best friend were sharing their story with you. Remember, in good times and bad, a best friend simply wants what's best for us, without a hidden agenda. When things are going well, a best friend is there to share in your happiness. They also stand by you through tough times and challenges. And, if someone is treating you badly or taking advantage of you, your best friend is there to stand up for your rights. Amber's friends and family recognized the issues in her relationship and tried to discuss them with her. However, as we know, Amber refused to hear their concerns and further isolated herself from them.

As you begin dating a new person, you are likely to be confronted by unforeseen situations that make you feel uneasy. When you are unsure of how to respond to these situations, you can use "The

Best Friend Test" to help you make a decision. The Best Friend Test is a simple litmus test where you imagine how you would support a best friend in the same situation. Think about your best friend and imagine that they are struggling and stuck in the same situation that you are faced with. What would you say to them? How would you advise or support them? Then, say these things to yourself and act on the situation. Fight the urge to use self-justification or to ignore what your best friend would advise, make the decision, and then act on it.

Using this test along with a promise to act as your own best friend will drastically reduce the possibility of entering into unhealthy relationships or situations. Your new perspective will foster a new awareness of your relationship with yourself and make it possible to recognize the things that are undermining your well-being, happiness, and success in all aspects of your life.

5
GETTING TO HAPPINESS FIRST: A SIX-STEP PRESCRIPTION FOR EMOTIONAL HARDINESS

Be single like Prince Harry—
Happily eligible until someone equally
amazing captures your heart!

For so many people who deal with depression throughout their lives, happiness can appear to be an elusive state of mind. But it doesn't have to be! According to psychologist Dr. Stephen Illardi, depression and anxiety are diseases of modern civilization. Ilardi, a renowned psychology professor with a background in depression-treatment research, explains that human genetic makeup is nearly identical to the genetic makeup of our ancestors who lived ten thousand years ago. Their genes equipped them mentally and physically to succeed and to pass on their genes in a world that functioned much differently from the modern world.

Nearly every aspect of the human condition is now different, including what we eat, how we work, and how we engage with our environment. For example, ancient humans were hunters and gatherers who "exercised" constantly, whether they were hunting for food, gathering, or moving from one place to another. If they were to eat, they needed to "exercise" for it—and our ancient ancestors certainly weren't eating Pop-Tarts and Froot Loops for breakfast.

Modern technology has advanced our lifestyles too rapidly for our bodies and brains to adapt. In addition, groups who live in conditions similar to our ancestors thousands of years ago are found to be much less likely to struggle with depression.

With these facts in mind, Illardi came up with his Therapeutic Lifestyle Change (TLC). He believes it is a way to gain the benefits of our ancestors' lifestyles without giving up the comforts of modern life. His method, which he calls TLC, focuses on how we can make small changes in our lifestyles to counter depression and achieve a healthier, happier state of mind, without the need for medication. Empowering you to be your best version of yourself, TLC is an excellent way to make sure that you stay happy and healthy even if you're not prone to depression.

Each of the six steps is designed to keep your brain chemistry balanced to help you enjoy your life and become the best version of you possible. Following these steps will make you more emotionally stable, so that you can maintain your own happiness every day. Let's take a look at them and discuss how you can use this method to get ready for your life ahead.

#1 OMEGA-3

You've probably seen Omega-3, otherwise known as EPA, around your local health food store and on the Internet, but what does food have to do with happiness?

A whole lot, according to studies. Not only does Omega-3 help to lower inflammation in your body, it can also change the way your brain functions.

Omega-3 fatty acids can be found in vegetable or fish oils. Due to its ability to help regulate moods through the neurotransmitters serotonin and dopamine, taking a supplement can assist greatly in the process of getting happier. These supplements are also an excellent alternative to commercial antidepressant medication, which may have unpleasant negative side effects on some individuals.

Serotonin and dopamine are two hormones responsible for happiness and pleasure. When you don't take in enough Omega-3 fatty acids either in your diet or with supplements, the circuitry for those two hormones doesn't function as efficiently, so you are less likely to feel happiness or pleasure.

Unfortunately, most of us have a diet very low in this essential nutrient. But the good news is it's easy to find as a supplement.

Ilardi recommends supplements that provide a daily dose of 1,000 mg of EPA and 500 mg of DHA for enhancing a positive mood, in conjunction with the other strategies listed below.

#2 PREVENTING RUMINATION

Another important goal is to prevent rumination. Rumination is constantly thinking of and dwelling on negative thoughts and ideas, and it is a destructive habit. It will only worsen your mood, and make problems seem larger than they are.

If rumination is the act of musing or dwelling on ideas and feelings, Ilardi's anti-rumination strategies focus on the concept of preventing the negative state that people can suffer in during depression. Anti-rumination strategies are based around looking for distractions from negative ideas and feelings (such as finding an enjoyable activity to engage in or spending time with a good friend), as well as transforming negative thoughts into positive ones (through writing down the ideas and feelings so as to move on and get past them).

It is interesting to note here that James W. Pennebaker, a social psychologist and language expert at the University of Texas, has observed in his research that when writing down negative ideas and feelings, *changing the story* is a fundamental component to reducing depression and getting happier: "[W]e found that three aspects of emotional writing predicted improvements in people's physical and mental health: accentuating the positive parts of an upheaval, acknowledging the negative parts, and constructing a story over the days of writing." Thus, changing perspective is a critical component to managing negative ideas and feelings, and can be a useful practice when engaging in anti-rumination strategies.

Only you can recognize rumination and put a stop to it, so it is very important to pay attention to your thoughts and be certain they don't reflect a negative mindset. When you catch yourself ruminating over negative thoughts and ideas, it is best to distract yourself with activities like exercise or hobbies. More ideas for how to prevent rumination are available on Illardi's website at the University of Kansas available at http://tlc.ku.edu/.

#3 EXERCISE

Speaking of exercise, that is another important part of TLC. Maintaining a healthy body not only helps to keep you looking good, but also acts as a mood lifter and a source of increased overall energy.

Regular physical exercise has a whole host of health benefits, including improving sleep and cardiovascular function, reducing stress and blood pressure, increasing flexibility and muscle strength, and more. When it comes to TLC, exercise makes a big difference! All kinds of exercise can be beneficial to the body and to a healthy, happy state of mind. Specifically, Illardi recommends elevating your heart rate to about 120 to 160 beats per minute for 35 to 40 minutes at least three times each week to maximize exercise for TLC purposes (and to use exercise as an effective antidepressant).

Types of aerobic exercise include walking (ideally at a brisk pace to achieve a moderate level of physical activity), jogging, and running, as well as swimming and bicycling. A large part of exercising includes finding an activity that you enjoy and have easy access to, so as to ensure that you will be able to stick with it. If you prefer to focus more on anaerobic activities, such as strength training or Pilates, that's totally fine as well. It would be better to engage in the activity you enjoy the most rather than try to force yourself to participate in an exercise you are not as keen on. Some form of regular exercise is better than none.

#4 LIGHT

Light exposure is something many of us don't think about much, but it has a much more important role in keeping you happy than you think. Due to our long ancestral history of spending the day outside, our brains have developed a rhythm that depends on the bright light of the sun. When we spend all day in a room, even if it is brightly lit, we don't get enough light for the needs of our brain.

Spending at least thirty minutes a day exposed to bright light, preferably at the same time every day, is essential to your wellbeing. This strategy is simple and easy to implement—and it can have quite the impact on decreasing symptoms of depression. For a cost-effective method, simply go outside to soak up the sun for thirty minutes or longer every day. If you live in a cold climate or if getting outside can be challenging for you, there are also "light box" options, which emit 10,000 lux: your own personal sunshine to enjoy at home! Be sure to make the effort to get exposed to light every single day to reap the most benefits from this simple get-happy strategy.

#5 SLEEP

Something all that extra light will also help with is a good sleep schedule. When your brain gets enough light, it knows you have been awake long enough to go to sleep.

A regular sleep schedule is vital, and making sure that you spend plenty of time sleeping is especially important. The National Sleep Foundation states that sleep is important for a variety of reasons. Getting adequate sleep can help with managing weight, improve memory and concentration skills, enhance our coordination, and reduce stress. Ilardi's research has indicated that healthy sleep patterns can contribute dramatically to reducing the likelihood of depression.

Many people take time away from their sleep schedule to make up for hectic lifestyles, but it is important to remember that if you do, you are sacrificing your happiness and mental stability as well. At least eight hours of sleep per night is needed to maintain the right brain chemistry to function well.

A healthy sleep pattern includes falling asleep and waking up at approximately the same time each day, getting a restful sleep based on your individual needs (adults generally need seven to nine hours of sleep), and establishing bedtime rituals. Since sleep deprivation and other sleep problems are often associated with depression, you may find that by incorporating the other five TLC strategies listed here into your daily life, a healthy sleep pattern will come into line much more naturally than it otherwise might.

Sometimes the best way to get yourself to sleep is getting into a habit before bed every night. Avoiding alcohol or caffeine in the evening, dimming the lights before bed, and staying away from harshly lit screens like the TV or your computer screen can all help you get to sleep more easily. Your body and your brain will thank you for it.

#6 BUILDING POSITIVE RELATIONSHIPS AND GETTING SOCIAL SUPPORT

Lastly, Illardi recommends having a social group you stay close with. Whether they are friends from school or work, family, or a social club, it is very important to keep people in your life with whom you can make regular contact.

It may seem obvious, but too many times we allow ourselves to grow apart from other people. We need interaction to stay happy, so those social connections we have lost along the way may hurt us more than we realize. Making a conscious effort to find and reconnect with the people we care about cannot only provide a support group but also keep us from struggling with loneliness and unhappiness.

A strong social community can help manage depression and increase happiness in a variety of ways. First, having good social support can help to increase your chances at succeeding with some of the other strategies listed here: doing group exercise or getting physical activity with a friend, spending time with a loved one as an anti-rumination strategy, or enjoying the outdoors—and the light exposure that comes with being in the sunshine—with family. And second, we are evolutionarily inclined to work in teams and socialize with our communities.

If you live with family or close friends, find enjoyable social activities that you can do together. If your family or close friends live far away, make the time to have regular phone calls with them and find other ways to stay connected. You can also join community groups, team sports, or local clubs to meet new people and widen your social circle so that you can cultivate strong, positive relationships with others.

The above six steps have already been proven to empower people dealing with depression to become their best selves. You can learn more about the Therapeutic Lifestyle Change method and Stephen Ilardi's work, as well as how to make this information work for you, by visiting www.psych.ku.edu/tlc.

As noted on the University of Kansas Department of Psychology website, more than 70% of patients treated for depression through TLC experienced a positive change, "as measured by symptom reduction of at least 50%." There is truly nothing to lose: through making small lifestyle changes by using the Therapeutic Lifestyle Change method, you just might get happier and healthier, pharmaceutical-free ... and have the opportunity to become your best self.

It is very important to make sure that, in trying to achieve happiness, we don't forget that the smallest things can make all the difference. To become the best version of yourself you can be, look at your habits and see: Are you setting yourself up for success?

Up to this point, we have discussed several important strategies that will lead you on the path to becoming the best "you" possible. Taking the time to work through and implement these strategies in your life can be the catalyst that ignites your happiness and puts you on the road to finding lifelong love. But while these strategies are powerful, some people might need a little nudge to get them going in the right direction. In the next section, we will discuss some of the available services to consider if you want some extra support on your road to lifelong love.

GETTING SOME EXTRA HELP

So you don't have the manual on "Finding Love and Keeping It", or the one on "How to Have the Best Relationship". To be completely honest, the manual has not been written, and it does not exist. (Well, not yet, anyway—who knows?) What *does* exist is a way to educate yourself on how to find and sustain love. If you haven't succeeded, don't blame yourself, especially if you're doing the best you can with the tools you have. But if you're finding yourself too stressed out about the idea of dating, then maybe you need a little paradigm shift and realize that there is help out there. You don't have to do everything on your own, you know.

"WHAT KIND OF HELP CAN I GET?"

HIRE A STYLIST

Can you take an honest look in the mirror and say that you're happy with what you see? We all feel insecure about how we look sometimes, but it's important to address those insecurities rather than let them bother us for the rest of our lives. If there is something that you don't like about your body, why don't you like it? Then ask yourself: does it *really* matter? If there's something you want to change, why do you want to change it? Will you be doing it for your own satisfaction, or for someone else's?

It's important that you get to a confident place in your heart and feel good about how you look. After all, your body is the only body that you will ever have. And when you're literally comfortable in your own skin, it's a lot easier to focus on other things that are beyond the physical.

It might give you some peace of mind to hire a stylist—or as they are often referred to these days, an image consultant, style consultant, or personal shopper. Get a new haircut or even a new wardrobe, if that's what you're in the mood for. The most important thing is that you do it all for yourself. Discuss your personal style with your consultant, and make choices based on your own identity. If you're worried about whether you'll be able to "pull it off," remember that people who "pull things off" only succeed because they're confident. So go ahead and own it. Your own body is the best canvas for you to express yourself. Embrace that freedom and have fun.

HIRE A DATING COACH

Yes, dating coaches exist. But before you freak out, I assure you that they can be very helpful. If Google didn't have the answers for you—let's face it, Google doesn't have all the answers—then maybe a dating coach will. Here's what they can do for you:

Generally, they can help you modify your journey to true love. They will be able to keep you in shape and on track to find it. Having a dating coach is like having a personal trainer. You use a personal trainer to transform your body, so why not use a dating coach to transform your love life? This will be a joint effort and collaborative process, and you'll have to remember that the coach is the teacher. You will be on the same team, and they will be able to demonstrate some better techniques than the ones you may currently be using. The idea is to break down the barriers that have kept you at bay and alone.

You might be a bit apprehensive at first, but when you see yourself closer to the finish line—love—any skepticism you once had will disappear. You will learn new ideas about who you are and will see things as they *really* are instead of how you *think* they are. This is a very empowering approach, and while not conventional, this process can ultimately help you highlight your attributes and strengths. A dating coach can teach you to identify exactly what you are looking for and give you pointers on how to get there. They will guide you on the fundamental techniques about who to call, when to call, when to text, and how much grace time is needed after that first date. They will teach you the dos and don'ts that will showcase your inner beauty and magnetic charm. They will help you discover how to give the best first impression and help you feel more confident. They can also help you explore how to navigate more comfortably in intimate settings. The coach will use their expertise and experiences to help you find love and happiness.

Getting to Happiness First: A Six-Step Prescription for Emotional Hardiness

Relationship and dating coaches are actually more in demand today than ever before. These days we are juggling family, work, and perhaps even school, so we have to do the best we can, given the limited time we have. Working with a dating or relationship coach can and will become a valuable tool. They will determine what you are looking for in a partner, from looks and personality to careers, education, and culture. They will bring the scout team in to find those who best complement you, balancing your wants and your needs.

If you do realize that this is the next and right step for you, then go ahead and let the fun begin! Together you will create your profile, which is like a resume for work—except this one will be your resume for dating, and it will be the tool you'll use to make your first impression. Dating and relationship coaches have a talent in creating and designing your profile in a way that is brilliant—and in a way that if you didn't feel that good about yourself before that profile was made, you certainly will when they have completed it.

Your first interview will be the "meet and greet" and will usually begin with a telephone interview. This interview will include a series of questions that will reveal a bit about your personality—who you are and what you are like. This information will let the coach know how they can begin to represent you in an area that may be a bit foreign to you. It is so important that you are brutally honest with your coach. After all, if you're not honest, then they won't be able to move forward and get you steadily to the next step.

They will definitely be showcasing your paramount qualities. If you're not seeing these qualities now, then your "Getting to Love" coach will help you discover them. They will also be there for you as you prepare that initial response to the first e-mail, "kiss," or "like" you receive on your preferred dating site. In this case, you begin communicating with your potential candidates, and if all goes well, you will have to continue communicating with them. If you have a relationship and dating coach who can offer you guidance and support, you'll walk through this journey like a champion. Also, the best part of having a coach is that you'll have access to them just about 24/7. They understand the importance of availability. And you will find that as your online dating pool of candidates grows, so will your choices for Dating and Relationship coaches with whom you can collaborate.

In the age of Dating 3.0 and the onset of "e-lationships," we must realize that there are many ways to find love. There is now less stigma associated with Internet dating. Fast and furious, slow and steady... It's all up to you. However you choose to go about it, the important thing is that you're comfortable with who you are and confident about what you're ready to offer.

SECTION 2
DATING LET'S DO THIS

6
DATING 1.0
MIXING AND MINGLING

Meeting your soulmate by chance encounter is ideal. For the rest of us, finding a soulmate is challenging work.

THE HISTORY OF DATING: AN OVERVIEW

Dating is a very familiar concept in today's culture, but meeting your potential partner wasn't always this casual—or, actually, this complex. Have you ever heard the story of how your grandparents first met? What about your grandparents' parents, and their parents before them? We may have seen the movies, read the novels, and heard the stories about attraction and dating in the old days—but how true to life are they? What was it really like before the cell phone, the Internet, and even the beeper? What was it like when handwritten love letters were all the rage? Your grandfather might often declare (and maybe kind of brag): "Back in my day, we weren't even allowed to hold hands!" Well, he wouldn't be kidding.

Dating in America has definitely changed over the last 100 years. Whether we have technology to thank or curse for this, we may never know. Now we send affectionate text messages in place of what might have been an epic quest for our grandparents just to hold hands in their day. Sure, the unwritten rules of dating have evolved and have possibly become more complicated. But everything is so much faster now, and it all seems so much easier. In fact, people are not just dating these days. They are "hooking up"—an idea that certainly would have shocked some people decades ago.

Let's have a quick history lesson and see just how much our notion of romance has evolved since then.

"WILL YOU GO ON A DATE WITH ME?"

Did you know that at the start of the twentieth century, couples were not even allowed to have any physical contact? They were never left alone, and it was only because it was expensive to entertain guests in the home that they began to spend time together outside. Mostly, they only used this opportunity to learn about each other on a more intellectual level.

And so the term "going on a date" came into existence. Couples were very exclusive at this point, and the idea of dating more than one person was not something that even entered anyone's mind. There was no sexual promiscuity, either—especially given the fact that their parents were present the entire time. That's right. Kids these days may groan at the idea of having a chaperone, but back then, a date meant going on a romantic picnic with your beloved while your parents listened in on your conversation. Yikes!

The 1920s were a more colorful time, though. The economy was doing very well, and people became more focused on entertainment. It was the time of endless jazz parties, and of course, the sleek (and much cheaper) cars to take people there. This onset of the automobile certainly made it more convenient to plan social activities, which changed the type of dating that eventually became more prevalent. However, during this time most women didn't work outside of the home and were dependent on their husbands to earn a living for the family. Because of this, single women were primarily concerned with the status of the man that she chose to date and eventually marry.

"LET'S GO STEADY."

When World War II took place, a lot of American men were called to enlist, until their population eventually grew scarce. Needless to say, the short supply of men was a bit of a problem. Women certainly stepped up during this time, joining the workforce and contributing their skills to the war effort. They also became less concerned by men's economic status and instead more concerned about their survival. Gay men and women who used to be isolated before the war began to meet as soldiers and volunteers as well.

And so, amidst the chaos of war, a new label was born: "going steady." It became a custom to show one's loyalty to their beloved by offering them a ring or an article of clothing. And because these were committed relationships, premarital sex was now on the scene.

"WANNA HOOK UP?"

The sexual revolution in the 1960s marked the end of the dating era and began the time of the "hook up." This revolution included the onset of the birth control pill, which came about alongside the Women's Movement. Can you say sex, drugs, and rock 'n' roll? You sure can. This was, after all, precisely the time when people began experimenting with alcohol and psychedelic drugs. The movement encouraged women to assert their own sexuality, and there was less stigma attached to sex. The rising popularity of the birth control pill also gave women more freedom to engage in sexual activities with more than one partner.

Meanwhile, the gay and lesbian rights movement also began, most notably with the Stonewall Riots in New York in 1969. The American Psychiatric Association also discontinued classifying homosexuality as a mental illness in the early 1970s. With these changing views on homosexuality, more gay couples continued to fight for their rights and began to form unions, though these unions were yet to be recognized as legal marriages.

"C U L8R?"

Dating began to evolve considerably during 2001–2010. Chatting, texting, going on dates—all of this became natural social activities for almost anyone. Meeting in person, whether at the bars, at coffee shops, or at the gym, had also become very casual and non-threatening. It became an individualized process separate and spanned across the spectrum, without any consequences to one's reputation.

And as we continue to explore varying concepts of gender and sexuality, so does our concept of dating in today's Web 2.0 continue to evolve. We have entered a world that is fast-paced and filled with authenticity and deception, commitment and disloyalty, intimacy and paranoia, obsessions and trust—and, of course, sex. With technology on the rise, all aspects of the relationship scene also continue to change. We are at the age of a reentered romance and serendipity, and whether we're holding hands or typing on a keyboard, one thing is for sure: We are remaking the landscapes of modern relationships.

7
DATING 2.0 AND BEYOND

Online dating can be abstract and impersonal; like trick or treating as a child: You see so many faces, that they all blend together.

One Friday afternoon, I fired up my laptop on my favorite table at Starbucks and got ready to begin working. This isn't my "home Starbucks," but one that I have often frequented when my home spot was overflowing. Perhaps a change of scenery was what I needed to jumpstart my writing for the day.

Upon returning to my table after retrieving my coffee, I began to focus on the document on my computer. Then a beautiful woman came into my peripheral vision and blew what concentration I had. She joined another woman, and they were now seated a few tables away from me. They appeared to be involved in some sort of business meeting.

Within seconds, I had made a complete assessment of this woman who stole my attention. Beginning with a scan of her bare ring finger, I quickly assumed that she was not married. She appeared to be in her early thirties, though I would have believed her if she told me she was twenty-eight or thirty-eight. She wore her shoulder-length blond hair down. Her beautiful blue eyes were big and bright. Dressed in business casual attire, she looked happy, confident, accomplished, and well put together. In her left hand, she carried a small Louis Vuitton clutch. My thoughts?

Wow.

As she began talking with her companion, I couldn't help but wonder if she had noticed me too. My experience had taught me that in an environment like a coffee shop during the day, women could only be approached if they seemed to be open to a conversation. I searched her for a clue, a hint, an invitation, even a friendly glance. I needed something to give me the green light to approach her and strike up a conversation.

So, reluctantly staring at my screen once again, I waited and occasionally glanced in her direction, hoping to make eye contact or even steal a smile from her.

As I sat there, I began to think about how I would approach this woman and what I would say. That's when the doubts began to creep in. At first, the excuses seemed to be perfectly logical. I figured that she would respond pleasantly to my being respectful. That's usually a good starting place, right? But then I thought about the fact that I would be interrupting what clearly appeared to be a business meeting, which was then followed by the fear that she would think I was crazy, or just a pig. Now it didn't seem so respectful in that light.

One by one, I considered each possibility as my anxiety about approaching her continued to grow. Was I actually afraid to approach her? Or was the situation just not appropriate? After all, this wasn't a bar—and she was in an interview or something, right? Slowly, my fears won out. Approaching a "perfect stranger" outside of a singles' activity or bar scene had never been easy for me. Even if she wore a T-shirt that said "I'm single and looking," I still wouldn't know how to approach her in an environment that was more a professional meeting place than a hook-up scene. I certainly knew nothing about her and her suitability as a potential partner.

So I did nothing, and she walked out and drove away in her BMW, leaving me with my computer screen once again.

Was it a missed opportunity? Maybe. If only there was a way to find out whether someone's single and looking without having to plan The Ultimate Strategy for that grueling five-second walk to her table . . . Oh, wait.

The Internet exists!

Even though some people still look at online dating with suspicion, studies show that couples who meet online report higher rates of marital satisfaction and a lower break-up rate. So online dating has a proven track record, leading to positive outcomes for the partners who meet this way. While it is becoming more and more a viable option, there are some things to keep in mind if you want to get the most out of it.

TOP TEN REASONS WHY ONLINE DATING SUCKS!

10. You just found out that your dad is e-mailing the same women that you e-mail.

9. You've been on so many coffee dates that even the Starbucks baristas call you "SexyKat34."

8. eHarmony insists that you go on a date with your ex.

7. Digital cameras are now high-resolution.

6. You seem to lose your beer goggles before every first date.

5. Tall, Dark, and Handsome is actually a five-foot-six, balding, and obese man named Chester.

4. Strangers are always pointing at you and whispering, "Hey, that person is on Match.com."

3. Siri refuses to go on dates and let you know how they went.

2. Chester won't stop e-mailing you.

1. Scarlett Johansson isn't online dating, but Martha Stewart is.

ONLINE DATING: THE ADVANTAGES

There are certainly a lot of preconceived notions about online dating, but we hope that everything we've discussed so far helps you in forming your own opinions about it. We also hope that it encourages you to give it a shot. If at this point you're still unconvinced of the amazing advantages of online dating, here's a short list that might help you change your mind:

- Internet dating offers its users access to an incredible number of available singles in your area. Unlike in the real world where you have no clue about another person's relationship status, you know that if someone's on a dating site, they're looking too.

- Because of the whole profile thing, Internet dating offers a great deal of information that can help you determine compatibility and suitability of your potential dates before you even make contact with them. Even the barest of profiles provide information regarding age, height, vocation, education, religion, marital status, and children. This is a huge head start compared to the non-virtual dating world.

- Online dating provides for a nearly anxiety-free means of contacting potential dates. Most dating websites offer users the ability to communicate interest by sending virtual winks, liking photos, adding potential dates to a favorites list, and the ability to compose an introductory e-mail message without fear of being rejected or turned away in public.

- Internet dating allows for relative anonymity and privacy. Two people can communicate via the website e-mail system and learn more about one another without having to ever meet or exchange personal information. If you learn that you are not interested in meeting a person offline, you can easily block that person from further contact.

- Internet dating offers its users the opportunity to meet without having to leave the comfort of home. There are usually chat features and, sometimes, live video options on Internet dating sites. And of course, there's always a chance to exchange numbers and make a phone call.

- If a face-to-face date is decided upon, the couple often already knows quite a bit about one another. This information can help to foster fluid conversation about shared interests or surprising and especially intriguing disclosures.

- Several specialty dating websites offer users the opportunity to meet based on religion, ethnicity, physical size, sexual orientation, hobbies, professions, obsessions, and even chronic diseases. Americans have access to literally thousands of specialty or niche websites with members in every state. In addition to the main objective of introducing singles that are interested in dating, these specialty sites often offer members a feeling of community.

- Online communication through e-mail or instant messaging can be a very effective way of learning a great deal about another person before you decide to make a live connection, whether face-to-face or through phone. So, online communication can be an amazingly effective screening tool for a number of reasons. First—in both good and bad ways—behind the computer screen and from the comfort of their own living rooms, people are often more comfortable sharing things they might not be willing to share in person right away. Of course, one should be aware of the possibility of exaggerations and embellishing stats, but also appreciative of the time, effort, and money saved by learning a little about your anticipated compatibility before meeting.

- Joining an online dating website allows single people to create opportunities for themselves and take control over their romantic destinies. Online daters are actively searching for what they are looking for, and have an advantage of being able to conduct this search at any hour of the day from anywhere, and even to be involved in multiple dating sites simultaneously. This has the real-world equivalent of being in multiple places chock-full of single people at once, which is, of course, not possible in our physical realm. Some do believe that this systematic approach takes away the mystical feeling of the universe bringing two people together, but again, it's all up to you.

ONLINE DATING: THE DISADVANTAGES
When the Website Works against You

When you decide to join an online dating service, you will be required to build a "profile" of yourself for others to browse. When creating your online profile, the website will ask you to reveal some very important information including age, height, weight, body type, exercise frequency, profession, marital status, religious beliefs, number of children, diet preferences, dating intentions, geographic location, income, ethnicity, hobbies, and much more. Much of this information is captured in data fields that can later be used in searching for a potential match.

Having access to a powerful database helps members to shrink the results of their search and target only those who meet their criteria. With regard to very important issues such as religious beliefs or parenthood, this search tool can be an important screen. For example, many single, never-married members are not interested in dating anyone who has children. These users will conduct a search that includes only single people without children.

However, matters of romantic compatibility and attraction are hardly quantifiable variables that can be determined by the black dot affirming your preference for country music over heavy metal. Consequently, potential matches are often eliminated based on qualities that may not be very important at all.

I was once told that a person doesn't have control over whom they are attracted to. While I'm not sure if I believe that, I am certain that I can represent myself in person much better than my virtual self can on a profile.

In-person communication is highly reflective and adaptable. Your online profile is black-and-white and static. I once sent an e-mail to a woman inquiring about why she hadn't responded to my initial message to her. In her response, she indicated that she was concerned by the fact that I had answered "maybe" to the question regarding whether or not I wanted to have more children. More specifically, she explained that her experience had been that men who have children and say "maybe" aren't interested in having children at all. In my case, nothing could be further from the truth.

On the flip side, I have had women tell me that they hadn't responded to me because they were not interested in having more children. Go figure! While having another child isn't on my list of priorities or a requisite for dating, I certainly would be open to the possibility of having another child if it was a priority for my partner. Unfortunately, my explanation cannot be quantified into a searched field. So, the closest response that represented my feelings was "maybe."

ONLINE PROFILES: THE RULES

Like so many others, when I decided to test the online dating waters, I was annoyed by the thought of having to write about and "sell" myself in a profile. Sure, it was easy to answer the demographic questions that offer you choices of race, marital status, offspring, and others, but staring at the white text box with a flashing cursor seemed somewhat overwhelming.

CREATING YOUR PROFILE

The first step is the most daunting. And it's one that most people hurry through. Don't be one of those people! Study after study press the importance of a good profile. Don't just fill out the minimum required. The less you put, the less likely you are to make on-point connections. When you're vague, people who are relatively interested in what you like will contact you. It takes far more time to find out that only ten percent of those people are true potentials than it would to devote an afternoon to making a meaningful profile. So how do you do that? Here are three broad tips:

1. **Be honest.** You're paying for a service that is supposed to help you find your true love, right? So what good does lying do? Yes, we all tell little white lies on a first date. We say we love things we only like. We say we're more adventurous than we really are. (Are you truly going to jump out of a working plane?) But don't say you love animals when you don't. Don't say you'd consider children if you know you don't want them. The more honest you are, the more likely you'll have success.

2. **Be open.** This is a tricky one. You want to give a good idea of the type of person you are. But you don't want to overshare either. When the profile template asks for three things important to you, don't give one-word answers. Write as much as it will allow you (or a couple of sentences if it does limit you). But don't go into your divorce or how getting fired from a job changed your

life or how messed up your family is. Those subjects are more appropriate when you're having a conversation and can put it into context.

3. **Spell-check.** Spelling and grammar are so important to the first impression you make. Writing in all caps, not caring about punctuation, misusing phrases (for example, it's *couldn't care less*) make you look either uneducated or lazy. Neither is ideal. Typos in text messages are common. Autocorrect is the enemy. But you have all the time in the world to craft and proofread your profile. There are really no excuses.

Not unlike writing a resume, there seems to be something unnatural about describing oneself. Go look at ten different profiles and you'll see how people find creative ways to avoid taking about themselves. Often, people will begin their profiles with statements like, "I've been told that I'm attractive, funny, organized..." Others will even start their "About Me" section with the words, "I really don't like talking about myself, but..."

One thing is certain, though. If you are going to be good at the online dating game, you are going to have to write a profile that is going to effectively accomplish its main goals: presenting the best "you" possible while attracting the partners that you are most attracted to. Essentially, you are going to create a presentation that is designed to "recruit" rather than just advertise you.

The job of a recruiter is often much more difficult than traditional product sales. The inventors of the newest widget are much more interested in selling as many widgets as possible without buyer discrimination. On the other hand, a recruiter is not only responsible for selling the position or company, but also for finding the best and most qualified applicant.

The online profile can typically be broken down into three or four main categories, including: sections to describe yourself, sections to describe the type of person you're interested in finding, and photos of yourself. Sometimes, personality-type questionnaires are used for determining compatibility by the website and by users who compare their responses to the responses of potential matches.

While these sections are meant to serve the same purposes for both men and women, I would argue that their importance on a profile varies significantly between men and women. Yes, there are two sets of rules that apply to the significance of each section on a profile. These rules are much more a function of the different realities of being a female vs. a male. Indeed, a woman's photos influences the attractiveness of her profile in the eyes of a man much more than a man's photos influences the relative attractiveness of his profile in the eyes of a woman. Yes, men are visual creatures and a woman's photos are the most important feature of her online profile.

"IS THIS FALSE ADVERTISING OR SMART MARKETING?"

Price tags usually end with the number nine. We are accustomed to seeing merchandise priced at $9.99 rather than $10 or $29.99 rather than $30. Logically, we know that only a penny separates the two prices and they are practically the same cost. However, psychologically we are more comfortable with the $9.99 price and somehow perceive it to be less than the $10 price. This is a common sales and marketing strategy that most people accept without thinking twice about it.

The real estate industry also employs a very similar strategy, albeit for a slightly different reason. Agents often make pricing recommendations based on ensuring that a listing price fits into a particular multi-list search. When shopping for a home, buyers may have a price range that spans as much as $25,000 to $50,000. For example, someone who can afford a $275,000 home would conduct a search on the multi-list for homes priced between $250,000 and $300,000. A home that is priced at $302,000 would fall outside of this search and not be found.

Similar to the examples above, a person who just turned 30 would not appear in a search that only includes potential dates who are between 25 and 29. Being eliminated from meeting "The One" because of a simple search would be sad. Am I proposing that you shave a few years off your age in your dating profile? Maybe! In fact, through my informal research, I have found that cutting off a year or two is common practice, especially for people with an actual age ending in a zero or one.

Don't price yourself out of the market! Below I have created a simple chart to explain this concept:

Actual Age	Age on Profile
30–33	29
40–43	39
50–53	49
60–63	59
70–73	69

I anticipate that many will believe this practice to be false advertising or even outright lying. Allow me to justify this suggestion and look at the circumstances when it might be helpful to employ this idea. As we discussed, your online profile is very much like a resume or job application. It is usually your first opportunity to make an impression on a potential date. Your job is to make your profile as attractive as possible while minimizing potential deal-breakers.

Realistically, is there a significant age difference between a person who is 39½ and a person who just turned 40? Just like $9.99 is essentially the same as $10, I would argue that the practical difference between the ages of 39 and 40 is nil. On the other hand, there is a significant perceived difference between seeing a 39 and a 40 on a person's profile.

When you are sitting across from your blind date and things are going very well, the fact that your profile says 39 rather than 40 is irrelevant. That's why I want to stress the importance of being authentic, truthful, and honest with anyone you communicate with or meet in person. You should be forthcoming about your age and let your date know why you advertised yourself a bit younger. If he or she likes you, they will understand and appreciate your honesty. If they accepted 39, certainly your actual age of 40 won't be a deal-breaker.

Like anything else, there is a limit to the amount of fudging or false advertising that is going to be acceptable to anyone. My belief is that 1 to 3 years is probably acceptable and passable, especially if you look good for your age. However, shaving 10 years off of your age is way too much. Think about it. Wouldn't you feel deceived and angry if your date showed up and you learned that their photos were taken 12 years and 40 lbs ago? It has happened to me, and I felt cheated and robbed of my time and energy.

Remember, the goal of online dating is to move offline and begin a satisfying and wonderful relationship. Clearly, that isn't going to happen if your blind date feels misled and angry before you even say a word. Your online profile should represent your best you and showcase the best of you today. Making a bad first impression is certainly not showcasing the best of you.

"WAIT! WHAT ABOUT WEIGHT?"

Most online dating sites will require members to describe themselves physically by electing one of several categories that describe their body. For example, a user might be required to select one of the following words to describe their body type:

- Slender
- Athletic and Toned

- Average
- A few extra pounds
- Curvy
- Big and Beautiful
- Prefer not to say

This is such an important category that is often used as a basis for conducting a search. Therefore, it is important not to exclude yourself from any potential searches while remaining honest about who you are. This category is also the one that's most often exaggerated or embellished upon.

When it comes to your profile pictures, there are some basic rules that most people know (even if they don't follow them). Those Do's include making sure you're in the photo, you're clearly visible, you look happy, and you look like you do now (versus a ten-year-old, thirty-pounds-lighter photo). The Don'ts are pretty easy too: don't include attractive people of the gender you're seeking (including family), don't use only formal pictures, and don't put your Photoshop skills to use. But there are more advanced moves you can make (and things to avoid) that will help attract more people to your page and, more importantly, attract the type of person you want.

Show yourself in your element. This is the biggest thing most people fail to do. What do you spend most of your free time doing? Are you a gym person? A nature person? A jumping-out-of-planes person? Whatever you are passionate about, whatever you always make time to do, you should include in your photos. But there is a caveat here. You may hike every Saturday. That's great. And you're likely looking for someone who is up to joining you most, if not all, of the time. That doesn't mean that you should make nine of your ten photos hiking photos. It may be a big part of your life, but is that all you are? And all of those photos are going to look similar. The idea is to give a brief snapshot of your life. When too many pictures are nearly identical, it's not that much better than nine selfies in a row. And, no matter what you're doing, smile! Women smile in photos almost twice as much as men, but that number is still low (only 56% of the time). If you're doing what you love, make sure it's clear that you're happy to be there.

It's not just about how you think you look best. If you're tired of reading vague advice about using "flattering" pictures, you can always rely on studies and surveys. This is particularly helpful if you are that camera-shy person who simply doesn't have that many pictures of yourself. (For the record, that's not a terrible thing. Plenty of people prefer to be behind the camera, and it's not going to stop you from finding your best match.) So if you're having trouble picking pictures or you're going to intentionally take a few for your profile, taking time to understand how people respond to photos can help you make the right choices. For instance, studies have shown that men generally find women more attractive when they're wearing red. Further, women looking away from the camera get the worst reactions. For the guys, men have been rated facially attractive less often than women. So, men, include more of yourself in your photos but keep your shirt on (shirtless shots get poor response as well when it comes to a dating website). But don't take it too far. For example, there are plenty of surveys that say the most important feature for many men is the butt. That doesn't mean you should make that the focal point of any of your pictures!

Caption your photos. Most websites allow you to caption your pictures, but few people do. I'd suggest going one step further and adding a caption to the photos themselves. As you'll see, the full websites don't function the same way as the mobile websites or the apps. The user experience is different depending on how you're using the service, and you want to ensure that people viewing your profile have the best chance at understanding the purpose behind a photo you chose. These captions aren't full stories about your trip around Europe. A location and a date are really all you need here. But this will reassure viewers that the picture is recent and help them gain better insight into you. It's a step that many people never take and will ensure you're in control of the image you're portraying.

Include multiple shots. You can find article after article touting the best and worst things you can do in your photos, but they often don't address the number of photos themselves. It may sound difficult to include five to ten photos, especially if you're a naturally camera-shy person. But it actually reduces the stress. The more photos you share, the less pressure you're putting on any one photo, and the more opportunities you have to show what type of person you are. For your profile-viewers, it assures them you're a real person with a real life. You don't want to go too overboard, though. We've seen reports that too many photos are as much a turn-off as too few. Sharing 100 pictures can say you're too much of an attention-seeker or more conceited than you really are. Ten is a good cap to have. That lets you offer a lot of variety without risking a bad impression.

Don't use photos to prove what you have. These photos aren't meant to show off your house, your car, or your job. You can talk about your career in your profile. And if you're reading this, it's clear that your purpose to venture into online dating is to find a long-term partner. For some people, these sorts of pictures are intentional. Men have heard time and time again that women are attracted to doctors with nice cars and big houses (and there are plenty of studies to back that up). By giving into that, though, they are trying to attract someone who is possession-motivated, and that's not a strong foundation to build a relationship on. Posting these photos can also be an unintentional move, though. Many people don't realize the image they're portraying, or they just don't put much thought into it. You may simply think that the best photo you have of yourself is from the day you finally bought your first new car and have the biggest, best smile on your face because that's a huge accomplishment, and you worked hard for it. But it's important to keep in mind that total strangers don't know that. All they know is that there is a really nice car behind you, and they can easily think you fall into the first group, the intentional posters. Make sure the photos you share are about you, not what you can provide.

Put serious thought into sharing photos of pets and family. When you Google online-dating photos for advice, these are the two topics you'll find the most conflicting feedback about. Everyone can agree to avoiding bathroom selfies. But what about sharing a picture of your beloved dog? Or family members you see every week? This shouldn't be that hard of a decision. The easiest route to take is to avoid them altogether. Again, you can write about them in your profile. There are sections for pets and family, and you have a lot of freedom to write about what's important to you. If you truly want to include a pet, that's not a cardinal sin. In fact, studies have shown that women are more likely to open up to a guy with a dog. But it should be a picture of you that happens to have your pet in it. Such as you running with Fido. It shouldn't just be a close-up shot of your furry friend. Family members, frankly, you should just avoid. Not because people are going to judge you for including a holiday picture with your loved ones. (They may, but those may also not be the best people for you.) You should avoid them because your loved ones may not want to be included in the profile you're sharing with the entire world. And that brings us to our next point.

Don't forget to protect your privacy. It's easy to forget that you're sharing these photos and quite a bit of personal information with strangers. You're focused on finding the love of your life, after all. Privacy has become a more common conversation topic the last few years so it's likely something that's already on your mind. When it comes to your photos, consider what is in your background. You don't need to avoid anything recognizable. If you're in New York City, a picture of yourself at Central Park isn't giving away too much. But standing in front of your apartment building, or a picture with the view from your bedroom window behind you might. It's not something that should keep you awake at night worrying, but it should be on your mind when picking photos that you share.

Finally, don't overanalyze it. This could easily have been a list of 30+ Do's and Don'ts. There are countless pieces of advice out there, and you are going to be your worst critic. We've simply included some guidelines to help reassure you that you're sharing the best photos. But at the end of the day, it's about putting up the photos that make you feel confident. And the advice in the rest of this book regarding your profile content and your communications will help you understand how the photos are just one small part of it. Yes, they are important! You know that from your own searches of other people's profiles. But they are not the be-all and end-all of online dating. Share what you're comfortable with, and you'll have the peace of mind that comes with knowing you're being yourself.

Also, look better in person than you do in your photos!

What? Is that even possible? Yes, it is! We all know people who seem to have a hate/hate relationship with the camera. Am I suggesting that you select less than flattering photos for your profile?

Well, ask anyone who has considered online dating about their biggest concerns, and they are likely to explain their worry about meeting people who look nothing like their profile photos. And with good reason! Nearly everyone I've asked has experienced at least one date who looked very different in person than they did online. Thankfully, most people use current photos that show them at their best. But still, is this misleading? Maybe.

Certainly, we all post what we believe to be our most attractive and best photos on our dating profile. After all, we are marketing ourselves and want to appear as attractive as possible. But is this really a good idea? Yes and no.

Let me explain.

Based on my personal experience, only a small percentage of people I've met look better in person than they did in their profile photos.

Fifty percent of the people that I've met look better online than they did in person. Most often, people use photos that are very flattering with regard to body size and shape.

Is this false advertising? Yes, it is, and it happens frequently.

Indeed, I have had more than a few of these experiences, and they are very disappointing. But more importantly, I want to share the emotions, thoughts, and feelings I had about the perpetrator after meeting them in person. Hopefully, this story will scare everyone who reads it from the thought of misrepresenting themselves with outdated or inaccurate profile photos.

MY LOVELY CHLOE

Chloe's profile was a beautiful example of everything that I was looking for in a woman. Her "About Me" section was very well-written, humorous, and painted a picture of a dedicated mother who was ambitious, independent, successful, and cultured. Chloe worked as an executive, but she also made time for things she loved to do. Acting was her favorite hobby and she frequently had small roles in movies and local theater productions. In fact, she used some of her acting and modeling photos in her online dating profile.

As Chloe and I exchanged a few email messages, I became very interested in meeting her face to face. But because of our busy schedules, we were unable to coordinate a meeting for almost two weeks. In the meantime, we communicated nearly every day, spending several hours on the phone or exchanging text messages. I started feeling like I really knew her and that our first meeting would be very unlike any "first date" I had ever experienced before. Falling in love with a person that you have never met may seem unmanageable or even absurd. But after my experiences with Chloe, I can certainly relate to people who get into long distance relationships with people they have never actually met.

For our first date, we decided to meet for dinner at my favorite Italian restaurant at 7 PM on a Friday night. As a rule, I wouldn't recommend a dinner date when meeting a person for the first time. There are too many unknowns. For example, until you are face to face with another person, you really don't know what your chemistry is going to be like. Having to sit through an awkward dinner is never a pleasant or comfortable experience. Instead, plan to meet for quick coffee or drink for your first date.

It was raining and windy the evening I met Chloe. The restaurant didn't have valet, so I used my umbrella to walk from my car to the entrance. I arrived about ten minutes early and was lucky enough to find one seat at a very crowded bar. I ordered a glass of red wine and started to check out the crowd when I received a text message from Chloe. "Going to be about 10-15 minutes late" she wrote. I replied "No problem, I'm at the bar." She sent me a second text at 7:15 stating that she was looking for a parking spot. Knowing that she would arrive at any moment, I turned to look at the entrance every time I felt the draft from the door opening. I was hoping to see her when she walked in so that I could stand up and properly greet her.

I watched the door for the next 15 minutes, but I did not see Chloe walk in. I glanced at my phone again when a tap on my right shoulder startled me. Turning around, I was greeted by a woman that I did not recognize. In fact, I assumed she was a random person wanting to squeeze into the crowded bar for a drink. After a second or two, I was confronted by the realization that I was looking at a Chloe that was 10-15 years older and 40-50 pounds heavier than the Chloe I had come to expect. Her hair was wet from the rain and pet hair covered her black clothes.

Despite the fact that I felt like running away, I decided that I could learn something from the situation and we proceeded to have dinner as planned.

It's difficult to describe the disappointment and awkward feelings that I experienced as I made small talk with Chloe. Rather than focusing on getting to know her better, my thoughts were repeatedly interrupted by questions regarding her motivation. Didn't she know that she looked nothing like her acting photos? They must have been taken 10-15 years ago. And, did she not realize that she wasn't the petite woman that she advertised in her profile?

Was she pulling a fast one on me, or did she really think I wouldn't notice? After having dinner with her, I still wasn't certain.

I tell this story at the risk of sounding superficial. I realize that a person's looks has little to do with relationship satisfaction. I also know that attraction towards another person can grow as we get to know them and like their personality. Perhaps Chloe could have been a person that I would have dated under different circumstances. But the feelings of being deceived and disappointed during our first meeting were overwhelming and I was definitely not interested in going out with her again.

It's very important to post the most flattering photos of yourself on your dating profile. This will definitely result in getting more attention and increasing your chances of communicating with more people. But it's far more important to post recent photos that accurately represent your current self. This is especially true for people who experience fluctuating weight.

If you are a person whose weight varies by ten pounds or more depending on the season, there is a simple rule to follow with regard to selecting your profile photos. When deciding if you should use a photo, take a moment to try on the outfit you were wearing in that photo. If the same outfit fits comfortably today, then using that photo on your profile is fine. However, if you struggle to button and squeeze into the outfit you wore in your photos, you probably shouldn't post that photo on your dating profile.

CHOICE OVERLOAD

Let's face it—most people are reluctant to try online dating. It is often only through the constant encouragement that many women, for instance, decide to take the plunge and give Internet dating a try. The potential benefits of online dating become obvious enough, and then a person gives in, even if it's just to satisfy friends and family. These people begin with the end in mind, the goal: to meet a great person online, take that friendship offline, and develop an exclusive long-term relationship. Based on the recommendations of friends or relatives who were successful on a particular website, new online daters post a few photos, create a quick profile, and jump into a search.

I remember the first time I checked out an online dating site. I thought I could just hop on a site and begin "window-shopping" like you can on most sites. Nope. Not happening. The dating sites require you to create a profile before allowing you to see any potential dating candidates. Only members can browse and search for available singles. Because of these policies, there are many profiles created by people who just want to browse and will never read any messages they might receive.

Without including any of my photos, I created a skeleton profile and included as little information as the website allowed. I even tried to use nonsense words and sentences to fill in those sections, but the website was too smart for that. After entering demographic information and stats, I was taken through a few pages of compatibility or personality questions, which took about ten more minutes to complete. Finally, I was able to conduct a simple search of available singles in my area.

My first search returned over two thousand photos of women who were within my age range and proximity. Overwhelming? Yes! Exciting? Absolutely! If you've been there, then you know exactly what I'm talking about. But for those who have yet to explore the world of online dating, be prepared to be overwhelmed—in a good way!

I remember how excited I was when I realized the opportunity and potential that online dating offered single adults. There they were: thousands of single and unattached women, all looking for the right man to meet and connect with. That could be me! It overwhelmed me to realize just how many unique and interesting people I now actually had the chance to get to know.

Never before have we had the ability to reach out to so many potential partners from all over the world. We now have so many choices. That's great, right?

Well, yes, of course. But not always. When you have too many choices, it becomes more difficult to make a selection and feel happy about it. And when it comes to dating and relationships, knowing that these choices exist can potentially make it more difficult for people to commit and stay committed to their partner. Choice overload is definitely a paradox of progress.

MAKING CONTACT

You have your profile up, and people are visiting. Great! The next step is to start interacting. People will message you, but you should also reach out to other people as well. This is what makes online dating spectacular: you don't have to put yourself as far out there as in the real world. If someone doesn't respond to your message, it's not nearly as awkward. You never have to see them. And there are so many people who are responding and reaching out to you first, you won't even notice the missing reply. For the shy people of the world, there is no easier way to make connections.

When it comes to messaging, the rules are pretty simple: Be polite, be prompt, and be real. Polite isn't hard. Most people are going to be respectful in the messages they send. And the inappropriate ones you can report and block.

Prompt is a little harder. After all, you have to work, you may have kids, and you have responsibilities. Most dating sites have mobile apps, but that doesn't mean you have to (or even could) stop everything to reply to a message. But don't let more than six hours go by without a reply. If you're really interested in them, show them.

Being real is probably the hardest. Again, we get to telling those little white lies. If you're asked a hard question that really speaks to the foundation of your potential relationship, be honest. Don't waste all your time, effort, and money on this site just to settle for something you know won't last.

One downside to online dating is that people can disappear, or ghost, without warning. But if we're being honest, that happens in real life all the time. It can hurt and be confusing, but there is not much to do about it. If you've been communicating, you can send a brief message that says you're here (if the person comes back online) or wishing them the best (if they don't). But really, the best thing to do is move on. You're likely getting new messages every day, and there are new people joining daily you can reach out to. Take advantage of your many options and recognize that you deserve someone who is responsive and caring.

TAKING IT OFFLINE

So you've been talking with someone for a while now, and you want to take things offline. There are a lot of options, and it really comes down to your comfort level. Many people share their social media profiles before their phone numbers. It can ease into getting to know more about the person before seeing each other face to face. A downside to it is that you're in less control of what the person learns about you before you've even met. Depending on how your friends post (and tag you), you may want to keep that step for last. One critical thing to always keep in mind is how they're reacting to your suggestion. If they aren't ready, don't push. And if they push you, think twice about sharing personal information.

Eventually, you must go out on a first date with people you're seriously considering. And the old advice is still the best: meet them there and choose a well-lit, crowded place. Coffee shops are great for a short pre-date where you can easily leave after a short while if you're not comfortable. Dinner is a bit more of a time commitment but can help people relax a little more since it's a more conventional date, something they're used to. Whatever you choose, again, be comfortable with it. It's okay to be nervous about this. Dates are always a little nerve-racking, and this is someone you don't have any references (for lack of a better word) on. If you want to be extra careful, don't pick somewhere very close to home and set a check-up time with a friend who has the picture, name, and number of the person you're meeting. But really, you should seriously consider your motives behind doing that. If you're a naturally overcautious person (it's a dangerous world after all), then go right ahead and make sure you feel as comfortable as possible. But if this is abnormal for you, then there might be something about this person that's putting you off, and you might want to reconsider meeting them.

In Chapter 8 Theresa will talk about the "first date" in more detail, but the same basic rules apply. Be honest and open. It's just a first date. If there are sparks and a strong connection, that's fantastic. But it's okay to think it's not a long-term match. If it's something to pursue, don't ghost on the other people you've been talking to. Be honest and tell them that you've found something you want to give a good chance. And then end all communication, put your profile on hold. Don't keep looking! If it's not something to pursue, be honest with the other person and end all communication unless you really feel you can just be friends (such as when you both acknowledge it is a terrible match from the start and can laugh about it). Then get back to the drawing board and start talking to new people.

THE IMPORTANCE OF SAFETY

This part of the book is of vital importance to ensure your safety online. You have to remember that dating and social media are entering a new age, and this comes with many risks. To limit these risks, we need to follow a few rules and arm ourselves with the necessary tools to keep us safe.

The first thing to remember is to *always meet your date in a public place*. Ideally, this should be where there are many people surrounding you who can act as witnesses in case things don't go as well as expected. It is also best to *avoid places where alcohol is served*, so choose a coffee shop or somewhere similar. And *never meet your potential date at their home or invite them to yours*. This could be very dangerous.

There are also many other things that you should be aware of which may indicate that issues will arise in the future. Being aware of patterns of behavior can alert you to these issues, such as:

- Is the candidate only available at certain times of the day?

- Are they able to change their schedule?

- Are they always working very, very late and are then unable to make the time you have planned to meet?

- Do you feel they have indicated too many times that they are dealing with personal issues and they just cannot get away?

- Does their profile sound too good to be true? If so, it probably is.

- Do you have the full name and number of the person you are ready to meet? Were they willing to provide their last name freely?

- If you looked them up, would you be able to find them? If not, there might be something wrong.

- If they begin discussing money on the first date, did they ask for any financial resources? If so, they need to be reported.

- Do they want to move the relationship on at a speed you are not comfortable with? It can help to evaluate that primary introduction to see if they are intent on moving at a much quicker speed than you are. A whirlwind romance might sound wonderful, until their tone becomes intimidating and they tell you that they want to start meeting in person right away.

- Are they beginning to make demands about the relationship before you feel you have learned enough about them? If this is the case and you begin to worry about their intentions, then please *go with your gut feeling*, because something is definitely wrong with that picture.

When people are using the Internet in the hope of finding romance, they sometimes tend to disclose personal information and have to be careful to not disclose too much or share information that may harm them. In order to ensure your safety, you must protect your personal information and data. While some of this information might seem insignificant to you—like a child's or pet's name—this can be an easy way for a cyber-criminal to gain crucial information about you.

Unfortunately, there *are* online predators lurking in the dark, and you have to be aware that they will be ready to steal any bit of personal information they can possibly get for purposes other than online dating.

For this reason, you should *never post your full name on any site,* and if you are not able to find any information on a potential candidate/date by conducting a simple Google search, then you need to *cancel that date.* If you feel more comfortable, you may want to *run a background check on them.* This is especially important if you have been dating and decide that the time is right to date them exclusively.

Online dating sites usually allow you to read profiles and review pictures when you are searching for prospects. They also have the ability to match you up with similar profiles and make recommendations based on this. Most of this information is offered at no charge. These profiles may consist of your first name or username, address, age, sex, education, profession, location of work, number of children, religion, hobbies, income, religion, and ethnicity, as well as information about drinking behavior, smoking habits, and drug use.

Other matchmaking sites will collect data by requiring you to take a quiz, a survey, or just answer a set of questions. All these sites are obtaining information about you so that they are able to match you up with potential dating candidates. However, you should also be aware that they might be selling this data for marketing and advertising purposes as well.

What is critical for you to remember about posting this information is that *once an online matchmaking service obtains your information, it has it forever.* In other words, even if you have already found true love and canceled your subscription, your information is still there. It now exists on other websites, and although you think you have deleted it, it sits on a hard drive or in a cloud somewhere, allowing others access. You can then only hope that it does not get into the wrong hands.

Photos are another area of concern. Just because you delete or update a photo does not mean that photo is deleted. Photos are uploaded into a separate network, whose databases are separate from the matchmaking sites. Therefore, deleting the photo might take it off of the dating site, but it still exists. In addition, when you tag someone in Facebook it uses facial recognition and creates a digital photo, which is placed in an additional database.

Finding a life partner online is very similar to a finding the ideal job online. Start with a good idea of the type of person you are looking for—the right fit. Then, find the online services that cater to these people based on interests, culture, location, etc. Consider joining several dating websites and visit them daily to ensure the best chances of finding your perfect match. If you were looking for a job, you would probably utilize every strategy, technique, or tool that you could get your hands on. And, you would probably search daily without limiting yourself to the strategies that you are most accustomed to or comfortable with. Just remember to be vigilant and safe. You certainly want to avoid meeting people who are intentionally misleading and not honest about who they really are.

Just as there are some people who refuse to use their credit card for purchases on the internet, there will always be some people who look at online dating with suspicion. Nevertheless, online dating offers single people great opportunities to meet and connect with potential dates. Why not create your own opportunity to take control over your love life today?

8
DATING APPS: THE NEXT GENERATION

Eeny, meeny, miny, moe? Which one are you though?

THE AGE OF TINDER

So far we've talked about how to get the most out of the dating websites currently available on the Internet. Many of them have a very detailed process in helping you find your perfect match, requiring you to spend plenty of time in front of your computer. But what if you're simply too busy or just don't feel like answering all those complicated questions?

Enter Tinder.

Tinder is a free, location-based mobile dating app that simplifies the process most dating websites would normally require. You just link it to your Facebook account (don't worry, it doesn't post anything without your permission), choose up to six photos of yourself from any of your Facebook albums, and write a brief bio.

That's it! Once you've set up your profile, you can adjust your "Discovery Preferences." You can select whether you want to see men or women or both, as well as set your search parameters in terms of age range and distance.

Then the game begins. The app shows you a series of photos of singles based on your preferences. You swipe left if you don't like them and swipe right if you do. You can also click on their picture to view their profile and see more of their photos. Because everyone's profile is connected to their Facebook account, you also get to see whether you have any shared interests or mutual friends. If someone you like also swiped right on your photo, the app immediately informs you, "It's a Match!" and urges you to begin chatting.

Beware, though: Many people have said that it can be quite addictive.

THE APPEAL

If you come from the world of dating websites, you may be wondering what the appeal is, and more importantly, how you can possibly find someone worth your time given what little information the app gives and requires.

For some, that is precisely one of the great things about Tinder and other similar dating apps. It's simple, easy on the eye, and it's basically a game. The objective? To find a Match and hopefully start a conversation with them.

It's more "efficient" in the sense that dating websites can take a lot of work, because most of them require answering a long series of questions to find the best matches for you. If you're not too serious about online dating, the process can get tedious pretty quickly. It's also easier to exaggerate or embellish information when there's more space for it.

Tinder, on the other hand, just gives you the basics and lets you work out the rest. But without any of the sophisticated algorithms that dating websites often brag about, all you'll rely on to make the decision is your own brain. Of course, it's just a matter of choosing whether to swipe left or right. It almost sounds too simple, right?

Well, not exactly. The decision-making process involved in using Tinder is a bit more complex than that. Making decisions on Tinder actually involves two stages: the rational and the emotional.

The rational stage is when you consider the factors of distance and age. This can be very important, because after all, it makes more sense to date someone who lives nearby and is within your own age range. It's more likely that you'll develop a relationship with someone who is nearby, because you'll have more chances of seeing each other on a regular basis. It's also more likely that you'll develop a relationship with someone close to your age, because you will likely have similar backgrounds, interests, and worldviews.

The emotional stage involves appearance and requited interest. In the next chapter, you will find a more in-depth discussion on how appearance (as well as age and distance) dictates who we become attracted to—but for now, we'll focus on how appearance counts in the context of using a dating app like Tinder.

Because the app requires so little of its users, it challenges you to be more creative. As I've mentioned earlier, while most dating websites require users to write a number of personal essays that share information on their background, as well as have more space for more photos, Tinder only allows space for six photos and a brief bio. With only six photos or less, Tinder users need to base their decision beyond how attractive they find the candidate whose profile they're looking at.

In the last chapter we talked about how to choose the right photos for your profile. So here's the question: If you were to choose only six photos of yourself to show what kind of person you are, which ones would you pick? Would you pick the one of you wearing a suit and tie or an elegant black dress? Would you pick the one of you surfing at the beach, or perhaps an artsy shot of you leaning against a wall while listening to music on your headphones? Whatever photos you end up choosing, chances are you picked them carefully in order to make a statement about yourself.

If you're the one looking at someone else's photos, you look for the same clues. A photo of someone on top of a mountain or at the gym can tell you that the person is athletic. A carefully lit and structured photo can tell you that the person may be an artistic type.

You will also find some hints about the person that they didn't intentionally include in their photos. For example, a long-distance shot or an obscure photo could mean they have flaws they don't want you to see. On the other hand, a close-up could mean they have a lot of self-confidence.

Once you've taken into account the candidate's age and location, gathered your clues based on their photos, and swiped right to say you're interested, the next step is to wait and see if they feel the same way. One of the main concepts behind Tinder is that people find it easier to strike up a conversation with a stranger if they know that the person is interested as well. If the other person also swiped right, that can certainly help you decide if you want to initiate contact.

And with the little information and only a few clues to work with, you'll have more to talk about on your first date.

THE NEXT STEP
"HOW SAFE IS IT?"

Because Tinder requires a Facebook account, it gives you some peace of mind to know that you're at least talking to a real person. Of course, it's also easy to simply create another Facebook account just for the app, but it doesn't take too much effort to determine which ones are serious about finding a match and which ones aren't. For example, if you visit someone's profile and find that they only have one photo and nothing on their bio, you can safely say that they're probably not that interested in making the most out of the app.

It's also based on mutual attraction, so you only get to chat if both of you swiped right. Many users, especially women, appreciate this feature, because it lessens their chances of receiving unsolicited advances.

However, as with any other social activity conducted with strangers on the Internet, it's still best to trust your gut. You may be on the app just to make friends and, even though you clearly stated this information on your bio, still find a match who only swiped right to convince you to hook up with them. Or, you may find yourself chatting with a married person. The important thing is to make sure that both parties are on the same page. And if someone is beginning to make you feel uncomfortable, don't hesitate to contact the company and report the issue.

"IT'S NOT JUST FOR STRAIGHT PEOPLE, IS IT?"

Tinder is open to all people of any preference in the sense that it lets its users adjust their discovery preferences and offers the option to be shown profiles of men, women, or both. However, some have reported that the app's gender settings still need some improvement. It's also possible that some people simply forget to adjust their settings properly. If you feel that Tinder isn't the best dating app for you, there are other highly rated apps out there that were created specifically for the LGBTQ community, such as Grindr, Hornet, and Dattch. OkCupid, which has plenty of users worldwide, also has as an app with great features for all people of all preferences.

"TINDER IS JUST A HOOK-UP APP."

The founders of Tinder say that it's an app for meeting new friends online, but most still see it simply as a hook-up app. Others describe Tinder as an app strictly to find a partner for a "no strings attached" relationship. Given the popularity of the app, I strongly disagree with that perception.

Indeed, there are plenty of twenty-somethings who are on Tinder for a quick hook-up. And, if you use it, you'll probably find a match who swiped right to convince you to hook up with them. But you'll find just as many interesting, attractive and successful people who are only interested in a committed relationship.

Over the past few months, Theresa and I have informally researched and evaluated the demographics of the typical Tinder user across a wide age-range (25–50) in various metropolitan areas including New York City, Miami and South Florida, Chicago, Los Angeles, Detroit, and Toronto. In these metropolitan areas we found that Tinder users were 55% men and 45% women with an average age of 28–30. Thirty-five percent of the men had photos only, with nothing written on their profile. The same was true for 30% of the women. Approximately 20% of men and women have also listed their Instagram user name on their profile. We also found that men usually wrote much less in their profiles as compared to women.

Most surprisingly, we found that when women wrote a profile description, they included some reference to not wanting a hook up at least 60% of the time. Let me repeat that: At least 60% of the time when a woman wrote something in her profile, she also wrote something about wanting a serious or real relationship and said she was not on Tinder to hook up.

Here are some of the examples that were copied from the profiles in the United States:

P.S. Not looking for a hook-up, but thanks for the thought . . . Makes me feel all warm 'n fuzzy, LOL.

Looking for friends and dating, not random hook-ups. If you are—again, swipe left. ;)

If you're not looking for someone to spend time with, swipe left.

NOT HERE FOR A HOOK-UP. KEEP YOUR STDs TO YOURSELF!

I'm looking for a relationship, not a hook-up!

Not putting out until we've got something really good going on! (That should get a few swipes to the left, LOL.)

Glamour model, fitness champion, marketing professional, mother of 3. I am not looking for a hook-up! In a relationship, but not married yet. Just feeling curious . . .

Not looking for "hook-ups" or meeting up with out-of-towners, but would love to find someone to go out with and have some fun.

Looking 4 a match, not a F*** B****! I like animals more than humans.

Looking to meet nice people . . . not here for hook-ups.

Nurse, single mom, independent, family-oriented, NOT looking for a hook-up!

Not interested in a hook-up, but am looking for nice, normal, employed, and hopefully funny.

Hook-ups, please swipe left. XOXO

Not here for a hook-up. A host to grab a few drinks and show me around would be nice. If you're cute, even better.

Not interested in hook-ups. I'm a classy, cool chick.

Regarding the male Tinder profile, 60% of them did not have anything written, and 20% of them had a tag line consisting of a few descriptive words or a sentence. We also found that less than 5% of the men mentioned anything about not wanting to "hook up."

While our informal research was far from scientific, I'm relatively confident in saying that women are aware of the "hook-up" perception, yet they are still willing to try the application in hopes that they may connect with someone who is also looking for a more serious relationship.

"CAN THIS TURN INTO A LONG-TERM RELATIONSHIP?"

These days we often find ourselves caught up in the here and now. We tend to have busy schedules and are more attached to our phones. This is especially true for younger people, who comprise the majority of Tinder's market. Younger people—although this is probably true for most of us these days—also tend to be more comfortable sharing things about themselves online. Indeed, meeting people online is no longer as unusual as it used to be.

Some say that apps like Tinder are meant for The Present. There are lots of people to "choose from" all the time, and it's a very quick process. It's also location-based, so you get to meet anyone anywhere you are, which makes it great for finding new people while you're traveling. And because it only takes a second to swipe left or right, it's a lot easier to forget about that cute person you liked who still hasn't liked you back. In other words, getting rejected doesn't hurt as much.

But say they did like you back. Now what? Can this actually turn into a long-term relationship?

There's plenty of discussion about the "seriousness" of mobile dating apps. In fact, many find them superficial because of how simple they are. Perhaps this adds to the app's allure and charm. Whatever the case, Tinder is wildly popular and has brought online dating to the masses.

People who have felt like online dating is desperate find it much easier to download the simple app, link it to Facebook, and begin swiping away. It's simple, quick, fun, and free—and everyone seems to be doing it.

Afraid of matching and chatting with a married person? Yes, unfortunately it happens on Tinder! Oh, but wait, it also happens in bars, restaurants, at speed dating events, and through matchmaking services. It happens in life!

Does Tinder make hooking-up and casual sex easier? Yes, if you're looking for it. But it makes finding meaningful relationships easier as well. What happens after you're matched, depends on you and your partner. Trust your instincts and make sure your partner is on the same page. If someone makes you uncomfortable, unmatch them, report the issue and move on.

TINDER SUCCESS

As a game-like application that connects two people primarily on the basis of a few photos, it's easy to dismiss Tinder as a superficial app. Clearly, your pictures are going to have the most significant impact on whether or not you are able to match and connect with others.

The way I see it, though, how you use the app depends entirely on you. After all, in this day and age it's highly possible to meet the love of your life through almost any method. What happens after Tinder will depend on you and your partner. If you both decide to delete the app once you've made things official, that's great. If you trust each other enough to keep the app for whatever reason, that's fine too. Whatever you decide, the key is in making sure that both of you are comfortable with it.

Today's technology, connectivity and innovative applications make connecting with and meeting new friends easy. But at the end of the day, you're still the one who decides who you find attractive and with whom you want to spend your time. Tinder is just a tool — a portal to connect and introduce you to others. But it's the biggest and baddest on the playground. And if you're in the game, don't you want to play with the best? Tinder is simple, quick, fun and free — and everyone seems to be doing it. If you're single and looking, keep an open mind and check it out. You might be pleasantly surprised.

9
BUILDING INTEREST AND ATTRACTION

Both men and women are attracted to potential partners who are wearing something red. Valentines are Red for a Reason.

Most of us have a relatively accurate understanding of what we are attracted to, and we recognize this from a very young age. For example, my first crushes in grade school were girls with blond hair and blue eyes. I remember how my father used to make comments about it based on my behaviors.

Have you ever wondered why you chose your last boyfriend or girlfriend? What causes us to feel a special chemistry with one person, but not another? Why do some people seem magnetically attracted to someone who is wrong for them, but feel nothing for someone their friends think is wonderful?

Let's start by defining interpersonal attraction. Interpersonal attraction is a person's tendency to evaluate others in a positive way, with the desire to approach them. It includes both physical and mental attraction as important determinants in human mate selection.

Who we are attracted to and how we pick our partners has been studied by psychologists for some time now. While we don't fully understand all of the complexities, research on interpersonal attraction has yielded several interesting theories. My goal in this chapter is to summarize some of these theories and explain how these findings can be applied to your dating life.

This task is easier said than done, because an adequate theory explaining interpersonal attraction and human partner selection does not exist. Instead, several competing theories attempt to explain interpersonal attraction from various perspectives. For example, one theory suggests that individuals will be attracted to someone who re-creates the familiarity of their childhood. Another predicts that the partner making the largest investment in reproduction, nurturing, and raising offspring will be more discriminating in mating. While both of these theories seem reasonable, they are certainly quite different.

Let's focus on the three factors that lead to the formation of a relationship:

1. Noticing another person
2. Becoming attracted to them
3. Interacting with them

Before attraction can happen, the two strangers must first notice one another. The second factor involves being sufficiently attracted to one another and having a desire to interact. Finally, the couple must have the means to communicate. The first item on our list is obviously the most important, because...

WE BECOME ATTRACTED TO PEOPLE WE NOTICE

The human brain cannot possibly be aware of all of the people we come in contact with. Think about the times you have been surrounded by large groups of people in a crowd, or stadium, or even in the shopping mall. If you had to notice everyone within eyesight, how would you be able to get anything accomplished? Luckily, your brain is much more selective in what it pays attention to, and filters out whatever is not familiar or important.

The good news is that our brain is amazing in its ability to capture our attention when needed. There are certain people who are more likely to capture our attention for good reason. First, we are more likely to notice unexpected people because they seem to stand out in a crowd. Our brains have adapted to do this because unfamiliar people might benefit or harm us. When they capture our attention, we immediately determine whether this person appears to be a threat.

Our awareness of another person is also influenced by their relative importance. Again, given our limited attention resources, we are more likely to focus our attention on those people who we believe have the power to influence our outcomes or help meet our needs.

WE ARE ATTRACTED TO PEOPLE WHO ARE PHYSICALLY APPEALING

Physical attractiveness filter – We are attracted most to people who are at least as attractive as we are.

A major factor of attraction is how a person looks. Appearance is the most significant factor that influences our immediate appraisal of a person. After all, we see strangers every day and immediately decide if we find them attractive or sexy within moments.

Several university studies indicate that viewing beautiful faces activates a reward circuitry in the brain, similar to the parts activated when having sex, using cocaine, or making money. This reward circuitry is activated by the neurotransmitter dopamine, and it gives the person a sense of pleasure. This might explain why attractive people seem to always find that others gaze at them—it is literally rewarding to do so.

WE ARE ATTRACTED TO PEOPLE WHO POSSESS DESIRABLE CHARACTERISTICS

We often like people, places, and things that are associated with the letters of our name.

Beyond physical appearance, there are personality attributes and characteristics that are likely to be attractive to most people. According to countless empirical studies, men and women overwhelmingly prefer romantic partners who possess intelligence, emotional stability, warmth, expressiveness, an honest and trustworthy disposition, and an exciting personality, in addition to a physically attractive appearance.

As one might expect, both men and women are repulsed by people who consistently violate social norms and rules of conduct. Psychologists call these undesirable partner attributes "social allergens." They include lying, gossiping about others, drinking to excess, and cheating at games. The list of social allergens also includes bragging about sexual conquests, constantly talking about previous relationships, or gazing longingly at other men or women. Not surprisingly, people also seek to avoid those who demonstrate poor grooming or hygiene, display poor eating or table manners, or invade personal space. Ultimately, we are attracted to people who not only fulfill our desires, but also avoid doing things that make us frustrated.

WE ARE ATTRACTED TO PEOPLE WHO ARE SIMILAR TO US

Shortly after completing my bachelor's degree, I was fortunate enough to spend a few days touring Naples, Italy with Amelia, an Italian language professor with whom I had taken several classes. We spent several hours visiting important monuments, viewing beautiful works of art, and exploring the city's unique cultural offerings. Because both of my parents are Italian immigrants, I had been to Italy on several summer vacations during my childhood. I had also spent time visiting family and friends in Naples. Still, no one had ever been able to describe and explain the city and its rich cultural and artistic background the way Amelia did. I'd definitely hit the jackpot when it came to tour guides.

During that trip, I remember seeing more beautiful people than I'd ever seen before. At first, I thought that I was being influenced by the way they dressed, which I found very sophisticated. By the second day, I was convinced that Naples was the home of the most beautiful people in the world. I mentioned my discovery to Amelia, who quickly turned it into a quiz and a lifelong lesson. To my surprise, Amelia didn't disagree, but instead asked me if I understood why I thought the people of Naples were so beautiful. Amelia laughed as I came up with various theories of better food, healthy diet, fashion sense, and even the possibility that I had a glass of wine before reaching my conclusion. Finally, I gave up and asked her to tell me why I found these people so beautiful. In her Italian-accented English, Amelia said, "Antonio, you think these people are so beautiful because they are just like you! This is your home, this is your heritage! This is what you know!"

On that trip, I learned something that psychologists have been confirming in numerous studies for years. We prefer potential partners who possess similar attitudes and beliefs compared to those who are different from us. We generally like people with similar ethnicity, socioeconomic status, and personality. It makes sense that people who have similar personalities would get along better with each other and have happier relationships.

Without getting too deep into the research, there are several theories that attempt to explain why we are attracted to similar people. The first area is concerned with perceived familiarity. They reason that because we are familiar with our own looks, those who look like us are probably more familiar than those who do not. It is this perception of familiarity that causes the attraction. The second theory is concerned with the perception that a person who is similar to us will respond positively to us. Lastly, some psychologists believe that we like people who are similar to us because they provide confirmation of our own particular way of perceiving the world.

WE BECOME ATTRACTED TO PEOPLE WHO ARE FAMILIAR TO US

The mere-exposure effect is a psychological phenomenon in which people develop a preference for things that they become familiar with. This phenomenon also applies to attraction towards people—the more often a person is seen by someone, the more pleasing that person seems. This familiarity principle was demonstrated in a 1992 university study where several women of similar levels of attractiveness attended a university class five, ten, or fifteen times during the semester. These women were instructed to play the role of a college student, but not interact with the instructor or any of their peers. At the end of the semester, students were given photos of the women and were asked how much they liked them. The women they had seen more often were better liked than the ones who had attended only a few classes.

Perhaps you have experience in the mere-exposure effect, or maybe you know someone who has had a similar experience. Personally, I have been in classes with women I hadn't noticed when the class began, but I became increasingly attracted to them as the class progressed.

WE BECOME ATTRACTED TO PEOPLE WE HAVE CONTACT WITH

Having your attention captured by an intriguing or beautiful stranger can certainly feel great, especially if that person offers you a smile as they walk by. You might get a quick boost to your self-esteem, but of course, the likelihood of starting a relationship with a person you see only once is very slim. Regular contact is an important ingredient in romance, which is why most relationships are between people who live, work, or go to school near each other.

Proximity has always played an important role in the way people start and form relationships. However, the advent of the Internet and mobile communication has made it possible to get to know someone without ever meeting them face-to-face. In fact, most of us have developed at least one professional or personal relationship with someone we have never seen in person. These technologies have made physical proximity a much less important factor in attraction and in the development of relationships.

While proximity has become less important, having regular contact of some form remains vital. Having more opportunities to communicate allows two people to learn about one another and encourages them to invest emotionally in the relationship.

As we've discussed, people are attracted to one another for a variety of reasons. Sometimes our attraction towards another person is based on his or her looks, but more often, we are drawn in because of their personality, confidence and familiarity. We are also enticed by people who are similar to us and possess the characteristics that fulfill our desires. Lastly, we become attracted to the people we interact with and see frequently.

In the next chapter, Theresa will talk about how we can put these attraction principles to use in the very exciting (and sometimes dreaded) First Date.

10
THE FIRST DATE

First Date? If you sell yourself like a car, expect to be test driven and comparatively shopped.

Sometimes you just find yourself agreeing to go on a date even if you're not really sure about the person who asked you out. Was it because he asked nicely enough? Was it because the look on his face somehow gave me the idea that it might literally kill him if I said no? Whatever the reason, the words came right out of my mouth:

"Sure, that sounds great."

There was no way I could take them back now. At least the dinner was still six days away—I still had plenty of time to brace myself.

I should have been able to see the screaming red flags he threw in my direction when he texted me up to three times a day and called me every evening before our date. Nevertheless, I begrudgingly had dinner with him, and this is what happened.

First, I could not figure out if my date had ever been on a date before. He seemed to break every dating rule ever created. He began our conversation by telling me how great we would be together and reminding me of how much we had in common. He also complimented me on how beautiful I was (well, okay, he had a point there). Truth be told, I felt like I was back in the nineteenth century and some people had secretly negotiated to arrange our marriage. "Did my parents put you up to this?" I almost wanted to ask.

Did it scare me, though? Of course it did, although "scare" is not the verb I would choose. I was actually turned off and mortified with all of the rhetoric about the future when I was just trying to get through a nice dinner and dialogue. I didn't realize at the time that there is a fine line between being nice, polite, and cheerful and trying to obtain a proposal before the main course is even served. Clearly, that first date did not require a second one. *Ever.*

There are two lessons to be learned from this story. The first is that if your gut is telling you to stay home and read a book rather than share a meal with a certain person, follow it! Second, if your date is overly excited to have dinner with you, chances are there is not much going on in their life.

Later, we will talk about some of the problem behavior signs to look out for, but for now, here's the big question: What should you do or not do on a first date—or in other words, how do you avoid messing things up before they even get started? Well, you have to remember that you only get one chance to make that first impression. Make that impression unforgettable, the kind that your date will actually remember fondly (hopefully forever). If you follow a few simple words of advice below, I am sure you will be at the top of the list of the best first dates they were ever on.

ATTITUDE AND BEHAVIOR

So you're excited to be on your first date. You can't stop thinking about the person. You've already planned your outfit and made a mental list of things you can talk about—not that you're really going to need it, of course. The first moment you felt that spark, you could practically already hear the wedding bells. And this could just be the date that finally leads to your happily-ever-after...

Whoa, there, hold that crazy thought!

Not to burst your bubble, but do not forget that *it is a first date*, and this type of thinking just might make it your last. This first date is just a clear indicator that both of you are on the same page in determining if there might be a match and chemistry between the two of you.

That's great, of course. But so far, that's all it is—a start. You will definitely need to be on your best behavior and prepare for Investigation Time, because while it's likely that you're both going to have a lot of fun, you will be judging each other during this time as well. So be sure to smell good and, of course, look your best—because the better you feel you look, the more confidence you will portray.

Also, if you don't like the coffee house or the bar you are meeting at, it would probably be best not to complain about it. This is all about first impressions, after all, so it's not exactly the right time to tell your date that you got into a fistfight the last time you were here.

Be sure to make those conversations flow. Try not to sit there as if you're being interviewed for a job. If they ask you a question, ask it right back. If they ask you if you enjoy a good basketball game, ask them if they do and if they enjoy actually going to the game or seeing it on TV. If you're genuinely interested, the best way to let them know is by paying attention to what they're saying.

Remember that your date is probably just as nervous as you are. They probably took just as long fixing their hair or choosing what to wear. So if they're showing you a good time, be sure to let them know that you appreciate it. Smile a lot. Laugh when they're being funny. The first date can be very nerve-racking, and you can help lighten the situation by offering positive signals that will boost their confidence.

CONTAINING EXCITEMENT OR NERVOUSNESS

Visualizing an upcoming date and the time you will share leads to increased sensitivity and enjoyment of the date itself.

The key to not being nervous is to use this energy to calm yourself instead. If you have created too much excitement at this point, you might end up disappointed. Don't build it up too much in your head. As they say, if you have no expectations, you may be surprised, but if you have too many expectations, you will be disappointed. Trying to know what the future will be with this date is ridiculous, unless of course you're a mind reader who can also time-travel.

Keep in mind these three possible outcomes: 1) your date may like the idea of a second rendezvous, 2) your date may actually end up becoming your spouse, or 3) you may not want to see your date again, ever. With three very different possibilities, you can't get too excited until both of you are on the same page regarding the relationship. If you're too invested and too excited, it might throw them off. On the other hand, if you're not excited at all, then there might not *be* a second date. Keep your eyes open, listen to your intuition, and remember that there is an element of balance and timing involved.

Before you allow yourself to get emotionally invested, think about it first. There might not actually be any sparks when you meet face-to-face. They might not even look like the person in their photo, or worse, it might not have been their picture at all!

You may have different agendas as well. While you're looking for Mr./Mrs. Right, they could be looking for Mr./Mrs. Right Now, or in other words, just a one night stand.

You might not be compatible at all. This can happen to anyone. You meet, and . . . nothing. You tell a joke, and they don't laugh or respond. They tell you a story, and you don't understand it or think it's appropriate. You may simply just not be well suited for each other.

You also have to ask yourself if you can trust them and if they can trust you. But of course, that's something that can't be answered after just one date. Only time will tell if they do what they say they will and if they do indeed keep their promises. Ultimately, the best thing you can do is to follow the golden rule: Treat your date the way you would want to be treated. Then hope for the best.

FIRST DATE TIPS AND SUGGESTIONS
Adrenaline makes the heart grow fonder, so take your dates on a rollercoaster.

Consider this. You only get to make a first impression once, and you only have about ten seconds to do it. That sounds a little scary, but all great things start somewhere. So make the most out of those ten seconds, and embrace all the possibilities they contain. Let's plan a strategy.

First, your physical appearance will encompass about ninety percent of that time frame. Your date will most certainly notice your smile and the tone of your voice as you say hello. A lot of it will rely on how you carry yourself. What does your presence or energy communicate? How's your walk? Do you slouch? Or do you have an easy stride that oozes confidence?

While you want to be perceived as honest, you don't have to be an open book. After all, you don't want to provide too much personal information until some trust has been established. When you begin moving to a more intimate level—and it is possible that you won't—this flow of information may be more acceptable. Until then, TMI will not be appreciated, understood, or warranted. Establish your boundaries. One good benchmark is to only ask your date things that you would be willing to answer yourself. If you think it's relevant or if your date asks, go ahead and share personal information as long as you're comfortable sharing it. But remember that there is an equally interesting person sitting in front of you, so use this time to get to know them. That is the main purpose of a date, after all.

While it can be very tempting to embellish, be careful not to over-dramatize your life as so great or so terrible. Instead, to put both of you at ease, try to establish some trust and transparency first. This will make the second date much easier. Find that line between confidence and arrogance, and don't cross it. Highlight your strengths, because people do like being around positive people whose glass is half-full. Walk into that restaurant armed with confidence and a positive vibe.

Always be polite, and regardless of how terrible the service may be where you are at, avoid being rude in any way. You know what they say about how you can tell a lot about a person by the way they treat servers? It's very true.

This isn't the best time to reveal that you dated or were married to the most awful person in the world, either—even if it's true that you dated or were married to the most awful person in the world. Instead, you can say that you are not dating at this time (until now), and that you learned a lot from your previous relationship(s). See the difference? Hint: one version sounds more positive and mature.

You don't have to let them know if you were married or dating Mr./Mrs. Wonderful or Mr./Mrs. Horrific, or what your sex life was like. If you have children, bringing up the topic will depend on whether the relationship moves forward. I know you love your kids, but do your best not to boast about them. Instead, let your date draw their own conclusions about them, if/when the opportunity arises. If the relationship continues, there will be plenty of time—the right time—to learn all these things about each other.

Be careful not to seem too lonely or desperate. People appreciate being around others who are happy, and it's very easy to tell whether someone is happy based on how they handle being single. It may also be a good idea to avoid talking about any illnesses or ailments. As long as you're observant, it won't be that difficult to gauge whether or not your date may be comfortable discussing a certain topic.

However, there *are* some hard-set rules. For instance, do not even consider talking about finances. Even if it's true, don't let them think that you need money or are in financial distress. Also, keep religion and politics out of this first exchange of dialogue. These very sensitive topics are most likely too intense to discuss with someone you barely know.

Other things to avoid:

- Being late. It sends the message that this date was just not important to you. Also, do not cancel at the last minute. That is just plain rude, and you may not get a second chance.

- Try not to be nervous—and if your date is, you'll only make them more nervous if you point it out. Don't be rude.

- Smoking. No one wants to kiss someone for the first time and realize that they're kissing an ashtray. Unless they're a smoker, too, then *maybe* you can get away with it.

- Garlic.

- Getting drunk. Who knows what you'll end up telling them? It's also inconsiderate, even if they're the nicest person on earth and offer to give you a safe ride home without taking advantage of you.

- Being ungroomed. You're free to be yourself, of course, but showing up completely untidy will send the message that the date isn't important enough to deserve a quick trip to the shower.

- No cologne, or too much cologne. While smelling nice can be a great turn-on for some people, others may be allergic to certain fragrances. Just try not to get too carried away.

- Don't comment on how much or how little they are eating. Don't be rude.

- Do not wear anything you would not wear to work. Something along the lines of business casual would be just right, unless you have both agreed to see a ball game or have a picnic. In that case, jeans are certainly acceptable.

- Do not discuss where they see themselves in the future. Stay focused on the here and now.

- Do not discuss love or let them think you love them or have admired them for a while. There is a 99.9 percent chance that this will completely freak them out.

- Assuming you already know that your date is not a sex offender or serial killer, do not ask a friend to join you this evening.

- Do not ask them if they go on many dates. Otherwise, you may receive the answer "More dates than you will be going on with me."

- Do not ask if they work out. If you have to ask, chances are they do not. Don't be rude.

- Do not insult or make fun of anyone. Being mean is a huge turn-off.

- Watch how your date treats the service people. Are they respectful, or do they talk down to them? If your date is rude to your service people, I am sure that is not the date you would like to be with. If they think they are better than anyone, this is not a good sign.

- Put your cell phone away or at least keep it on vibrate. Don't be rude. If your date is continually on the phone, texting and not paying any attention to you, they are being rude.

- If your date has told you they were a certain height or weight and you end up with Yoda, this is certainly something to look out for. If they said they were a certain age and used their high school graduation picture (taken in 1960), who knows what else they could be lying about? Some of them might be small and insignificant, but they are still lies and you have to watch for this pattern.

- If you are a man who is dating a woman—while it's commonly expected that the man should pay for the first date, your date may still offer to pay. If she insists on paying or splitting the bill, accept her offer. It won't make you any less of a gentleman.

To summarize, you have to take charge of your first date by presenting yourself as the charming, sought-after, and desirable person that you are. Discuss and share the things that are positive about you, your work, your friends, and your hobbies. Tell them how you have fun on weekends, and be open to learning about your date. What are their likes and dislikes? What are their interests? If you try to always bring the focus back to them and on them, you just might get that second date.

11
FIRST DATE FOLLOW-UP

Sometimes the first date that you aren't excited about becomes the one that is the most amazing!

TAKE YOUR TIME

While the first date is exciting, so is that first month. The anticipation alone can carry you through. However, be careful about making too many plans or making plans too far off. Do not jump ahead too much, unless you're ready to swim in that freezing pool of disappointment. This should be a very easygoing, fun, and exciting time, and no pressure should be put on either party during this initial stage. If you begin dating and things seem to be going well, as crazy about your date as you are, don't drop the L-bomb too soon. Take things slowly, or you might seem too desperate. Keeping things at "like" will let your date know that you are interested in them and in moving the relationship forward.

During this initial stage, it might be fun to meet up with some friends; however, I would caution you to not introduce your new friend to your family or children just yet. You need to continue getting to know them and know where the relationship is going before your parents do.

Because the relationship is only beginning, this is not yet the right time to offer a key to your home, show up at their work, or invest in purchasing something together. This type of commitment request might only overwhelm them. Also, regardless of how much you may need it, never ask your date to borrow money. This is dating suicide, and it puts you into a commitment that will certainly turn them off. Remember that you cannot ask your date to reschedule their life at the 30-day mark for you. You need to continue going out with your friends and keep your own life and the various plans that you have. And when the dates end, do not ask when the next date will be. Leaving things a bit mysterious only adds to your allure. Nevertheless, the idea is to take your time. No matter how well the relationship may be going, nothing feels better than discovering that you are on the same page and knowing for sure that you have "earned" these commitment milestones together.

MOST DATES WILL NOT TURN INTO A RELATIONSHIP

Some people enter your life as a blessing, and other people exit your life as a lesson.

You know what they say: It takes kissing a lot of frogs before you find your prince or princess. By now you probably already know that dating takes a lot of trial and error, and most dates do not turn into a relationship. But I do have a few tips on how to better these odds.

Try to have fun on your first date. Skip that coffee or dinner-and-movie, and do something a little out of the ordinary. It's difficult to talk to someone during a movie, and if the movie wasn't that interesting or was a bomb, then what? There are many other things to do, like cook dinner together, go miniature golfing or bowling, rock-climbing, or even go to the zoo—anything that the two of you can do together and laugh about. Set the stage to have some fun.

Who's planning your next date? If you are not sure you are going on one, then chances are you are not. Do you feel like you are? What is your gut telling you? Unless you are firmly set on where and when the next date is, simply leave the plans up to whomever is paying.

Evaluate that first date by reviewing the following:

- What did your date look like? Did they have good hygiene? Clean breath, clean fingernails, and no stains on their clothing? Were their clothes ironed and crisp?

- Did they have good eye contact, and did they really listen to you? What did their body language tell you? Were they leaning in?

- Did your date display good manners? Did they offer to open the doors for you or carry your things? And if you said that you could manage to do it yourself, did they back off? Or if they let you do these things for them, did they say thank you?

- At the restaurant, how did your date treat the wait staff, the valet, and all of the servers that evening? If there was a hiccup, did they remain calm in all situations?

- Did you feel any chemistry between the two of you, and did you play a bit off of this? Did you have good banter? Did your conversations have a natural flow that was sprinkled with humor? Did they attempt to make you laugh? Was the mood light?

- What level of confidence did your date have? Were they nervous? How was their posture? How was their walk? Were they positive and did they seem happy to be there with you, or were they constantly checking their phone or watch?

- Overall, what type of impression did your date leave on you? What if you were to never see them again? Might you be depressed, or would it be a godsend? Do they have friends, or did they not speak of any? Did they make a decision (like choice of restaurant) when they needed to, or were they at a loss for what needed to be done?

These are many questions in various areas, but they're questions that need answers. You have to take all of this into account so that you may discern whether there is potential in this person. From this data, you will be able to determine if there could be a second date or a third date—or, who knows, maybe even a relationship.

IT WENT WELL! NOW WHAT?

Dating? Eagerness is often interpreted as Neediness. Take your time.

One of the most difficult parts of the first date is determining if there is a second date after you have parted. Do you let them know what a wonderful time you had, or leave it alone and wait for them to let you know? Do you call them, text them, or leave it alone? Well, you have to do *something*, and you have to do it within the grace period. You don't necessarily have to wait up to three days anymore. You can just text them, which actually might be the best idea, especially if this was the method of communication prior to your actual first date. It might be a simple text message to let them know you had a good time. The advantage of sending a text message is that it allows the receiver enough time to respond on their own terms.

Should this message also ask about going out again? Would this be too soon? The answer is no, and if you did not ask for that second date while you were on the first one, then you may have missed the boat. At least determine if they would like to get together again soon for and do something fun. If you did not bring up getting together on the first date, then the text message is in order, and the next day or day after is acceptable. If you do not hear back from your date, then you need to end it here. Save time, energy, and your feelings. If you *do* receive a response, then *bingo!* You will be planning your second date.

Moving forward to the next question: When does this become a relationship? When can we *call* it a relationship? This will vary, and you will first need to determine if they are seeing someone else. If they are, then this may not work as an exclusive relationship. However, they might want to become exclusive, and if they do, let's hope you find out soon enough. If they want to date two or more of you, then it will be up to you to accept this or not. You will also have to look at some essential areas of interest. These areas may include religion, wanting children, having criminal records, or certain habits such as smoking, alcohol, or drugs. Go back to your list of deal-breakers. What can and what can't you live with?

If you are not interested in your date, you will still need to text them or respond to them. There are a few ways you can do this. The first is to thank them for a wonderful dinner and a great time, and then leave it open-ended for them to respond and let you know if they want to take it to the next level. If you do not receive a response, then you need to reach out only one more time. One post-date communicative follow-up should be enough, and if they do not respond, it is not because they did not receive the message—it is because they are done with the communication. So if this happens, cut your losses right then and there.

To get out of the second date, you may simply text them and tell them thank you and best wishes or take care, or that you will see them around. This will be enough to send the message that you are not interested in that second date. Keep it short and sweet, and then look forward to meeting a better match for you.

', '# SECTION 3

FROM DATING TO RELATIONSHIPS

12
DATING AND NEW RELATIONSHIPS

A new relationship is like beginning a road trip; awareness of the hazards along the road makes for a safer journey.

With the massive amount of options you have for dating today, you will have to determine what option is best for you. There is no one-structure-fits-all—you will have to see for yourself which one is right for you. Whether you meet by chance encounter, are introduced by someone you trust, or find a potential new partner through work, school, or online, the goals are usually the same: We want to meet, date, fall in love, and have a monogamous relationship. Regardless of how you meet, what is inherently important to the development of these relationships is *trust*. This is the fundamental and essential ingredient for a healthy relationship. After all, the foundation that we develop at an early age is a sense of safety. As children, our families provide this for us, and when we feel safe, we are able to trust. However, when we feel neglected or abandoned, trust can become more of an issue later in our lives and in our relationships. Trust—or the lack of it—will have a profound impact on how we treat others. If we don't have the ability to trust, we won't be emotionally available to our partners. And if we are emotionally unavailable while in a committed relationship, then the relationship is doomed.

With this in mind, we've outlined some of the most common relationship red flags to be aware of.

RELATIONSHIP RED FLAGS

It takes two seconds to say "I Love You," but every day to prove it. Gianna Borrello

A healthy and loving relationship blooms only between two healthy, loving, and interested individuals who are ready for a commitment. These four conditions are necessary for the development of an ideal relationship, yet many relationships form between people who are lacking in one or more of these areas. As a result, the relationship is less satisfying and more problematic from day one. And usually, one person is much more dissatisfied because of their partner's deficit or problem. Sometimes the unhappy partner even becomes obsessed with trying to fix the problem, and they're the one who seeks the advice of friends, family, and ... Internet psychologists ...

Luckily, most relationship issues are relatively common and are shared by many struggling couples. One only has to change the names and the faces to end up with nearly identical red flags, problems, and stories. And because the problems and stories are the same, the solutions tend to be the same as well. In this section, we will take a look at some of the more common issues that dating couples struggle with. I'm sure that you will be able to relate to many of these issues yourself. I certainly have. In fact, I've personally experienced every one of these dating issues at one time or another.

WHEN SOMEONE'S JUST NOT THAT INTO YOU

Don't waste a moment worrying about the person who isn't showing as much interest as you are. You deserve a person who's excited about you and eagerly checks their phone in hopes of seeing a text from you.

New relationships can be hypnotizing when you really like the person you're dating. The feelings are so electrifying that Disney created a new word to describe it in the 1942 movie *Bambi*. Twitterpated: an enjoyable disorder characterized by feelings of excitement, giddiness, anticipation, high hopes, and physical overstimulation, which all occur when experiencing a new love.

Something magical actually happens to your mind as you become consumed with thoughts of that person.

Suddenly, someone who was a complete stranger a few weeks ago is now the person that you think about the most. You catch yourself daydreaming and replaying your favorite memories with them, and you have to frequently direct your thoughts back to the present. Every detail of your communication and interaction is practically etched into your memory because you've thought about it so much!

Have you been lucky enough to have those wonderful memories and exciting feelings? If you have, then you know how exhilarating it can be. Let's take a few minutes to explore those feelings and understand how they are played out in new relationships.

For a few moments, I want you to remember a time when you were so thrilled after a date that you practically fell asleep that night still thinking about that person, only to continue fantasizing about them right the next day. Perhaps you can remember how you felt after your first date with a boyfriend or girlfriend with whom you eventually fell in love. Bring yourself to re-experience those intoxicating feelings brought on by the excitement of having someone you really liked. Try to imagine those memories and feel the emotions again for a few minutes, as if the date only happened last night.

Okay, got it? Now don't let go of those feelings just yet! I want you to stay in that happy place, and then answer these questions:

- Would you feel very eager to talk to that person?

- Would you be thinking about and hoping for a phone call or text message from that person?

- Would you be checking your phone and rereading the messages that you've already exchanged?

- Would you re-listen to a sweet voice message from that person?

If you are anything like me, you would have answered "yes" to all of these questions. Back then, some of you may have had to consciously remind yourself to focus, because your mind kept going back to that person. Or your friends may have even had to practically beg you to stop talking about your date all day. You may have even had to stop yourself from texting or calling the person. Getting the picture here? Okay, let's move on to some additional questions. I want you to go back to that happy place and answer the following:

- If you specifically told the person that you would call them or text them the next day, is it possible that you might forget and not text them?

- If you've been eagerly thinking about your date all day and they send you a "hello, how's your day going?" text message, could anyone stop you from responding to it?

- If you have another date planned and your baby-sitter cancelled on you, would you forget to ask to reschedule the date?

If you were really interested in another person, you would obviously answer "no" to all of these questions. It would be *impossible* to forget to call that person. In fact, you probably already planned the time you were going to call and what you were going to say! And if that person did send you a text message first, you'd most likely be beaming with excitement and waiting for just enough time to pass so you don't appear to be glued to your phone. Certainly, you would be happy to return the message. After all, you wouldn't want to do anything that might disappoint the other person or jeopardize the possibility of continuing the relationship.

Dating—or any relationship—is like an energetic dance between two people. When one steps forward, the other steps back. Then one steps back and their partner steps forward. A beautiful dance involves the coordinated energy of both partners who want to dance well together. One partner can't do all of the dancing for the other partner. It just won't work!

The same holds true for beginning relationships. Both partners should be engaging in behaviors that let their partner know how valuable and important the relationship is. When you really like someone, you want to know that your feelings are reciprocated—so you show them how much you like them and hope to receive the same level of attention in return. And because you want them to like you back, you treat them with as much affection and consideration as you can. And that is exactly what you should expect in return. If you've ever started dating or wanted to date someone who hasn't fully reciprocated your feelings, then you understand how frustrating and challenging the situation can be.

Anyone who is actively dating is going to have these experiences, and it won't feel good. But what's important is that you are able to quickly recognize when your feelings aren't being reciprocated—and once you're aware, to adjust your behaviors and your feelings accordingly. There's no need to spend your time worrying about the person who isn't showing as much interest as you are. There's certainly no need trying to understand why they aren't as into you. The only truth is that you will never know the truth, and it doesn't matter anyway. Just move forward and meet someone who is just as eager about a relationship as you are. Don't settle for anything less. You deserve a person who's excited about you and knows exactly how to show it.

DATING A PERSON WHO'S ALWAYS "TOO BUSY"

Stop making excuses for them! No matter how "busy" a person is, if they care, they will always find time for you.

Creating a meaningful relationship is not a passive experience. It requires time, energy, and attention to get to know your partner and develop an emotional connection. The good news is that people who like each other want to spend as much time together as possible. Couple time is our "relationship currency," which is why we say we "spend time together." Investing time in the relationship allows the couple to share intimacy, which is essential to develop a strong emotional attachment.

As you might expect, not all "relationship time" is created equally. For most couples, two kinds of time are important: activity time and relationship time. Activity time includes time spent in some shared activity such as hanging out with friends or family, going to a movie, participating in a sporting event, or working on a project together. Spending activity time with your partner means that you are physically together, but are not particularly focused on the relationship.

Relationship time is different. This is usually the couple's alone time where they are free to express physical and emotional intimacy. Relationship time includes time spent working on the relationship by "being there" for each other and interacting on a personal level. Discussing expectations, issues, and even resolving conflicts or arguments are also examples of relationship time.

Developing a successful relationship requires an abundance of *both* activity time and relationship time. Yet sometimes couples begin new relationships despite the fact that one of them lacks sufficient available time to devote to the relationship. Beginning this way tends to result in one partner feeling unsatisfied with the relationship, while the other feels pressured and frustrated. Let's look at an example.

Sarah is a 27-year-old teacher with a master's degree in elementary education. She completed her post-graduate education last year and has established tenure at a local school where she teaches second grade. Sarah is loved by her students and has been recognized as one of the school's best teachers.

Of course, she had to work very hard to get to where she is today. Back when she was still a new teacher, Sarah worked many extra hours before and after school preparing lesson plans, tests, and lectures. She was also enrolled in graduate school and attended classes two nights a week and on Saturdays. Her dedication to her education and career goals was very time-consuming and left little for her boyfriend of three years. As a result, her boyfriend frequently complained about her lack of time, and their relationship suffered. Not long before the end of her first year as a teacher, Sarah's boyfriend ended their relationship and started dating a woman he met at work. The breakup was difficult for Sarah, but she immersed herself in work and school, confident in the belief that her love life would take care of itself.

A few years later, having already accomplished her academic and career goals, Sarah finally allowed herself to consider dating again. She thought that it was the perfect time to focus on developing a loving relationship, which would hopefully lead to marriage and a family. She hadn't been in a serious relationship for a number of years, but she was convinced that it was only a matter of time before she finally met her future husband. And that's when she met Justin on a mobile dating application.

Justin was a handsome 28-year-old attorney who loved to work out and play hockey a few nights a week. Justin's job was very demanding, and he often worked late into the evening when important cases were assigned to him. He was determined to advance his career and was willing to work as many hours as needed.

When Justin received the notification from Sarah, he immediately opened her profile and began looking at her photos. He found her very attractive. For the rest of the evening, the two communicated via the application, sharing their personal stories and experiences. The next day, Justin asked Sarah to join him for dinner on Saturday evening. Sarah was thrilled and immediately accepted the offer, although she secretly thought that waiting until Saturday felt like such a long time. Justin ended their conversation by telling Sarah that he was excited about the date and that he would talk to her soon.

Sarah was so excited about her date plans that she spent most of the following day looking at Justin's photos and imagining what their date would be like. She wondered about whether or not he would call or text her. She set her phone to vibrate and kept it in her pocket all day. She also checked her wireless signal many times to make sure that she was able to receive texts or phone calls while in her classroom. The hours went by slowly as she continued to wait, until she finally had to leave school at 4:30 p.m., terribly disappointed that she still hadn't heard from him.

It was only until the day before their scheduled date that he finally sent a text message to confirm their plans and decide on a meeting place.

The dinner date went very well, and both Justin and Sarah seemed to have really enjoyed themselves. They had some great conversations, and Sarah felt that they had very much in common. The date ended with a romantic kiss, and Justin walked Sarah to her car. He said goodbye, told her that he enjoyed their dinner, and asked her to please drive carefully.

As soon as Justin pulled away in his car, Sarah immediately called her best friend to tell her what a great time she had with Justin and how much she liked him. However, it worried her that he hadn't asked her out for a second date. So she decided to send Justin a text message when she arrived at home to let him know that she was safe and to thank him for the dinner. When she did not get a return text from Justin, Sarah became increasingly anxious and wondered if he really had a good time.

Justin texted Sarah a few days later and asked her to go out with him again the following weekend. Sarah really wanted to communicate with Justin on a daily basis, but her friends insisted that she shouldn't always be the one to initiate contact. As a result, she rarely communicated with him between their planned dates. After their third date, Sarah invited Justin into her apartment for a nightcap. One thing led to another, and the couple ended up having sex. Sarah had hoped that Justin would spend the night, but he told her that he had to be up early and left her house a few hours later.

At this point, Sarah really liked Justin and thought that he was a great guy. She was very attracted to him, and she felt that they had great chemistry. She admired his passion for his work and thought that he was very intelligent. But at the same time, she found herself wondering how Justin felt about her. She yearned for a closer friendship and more time together. After a few more dates, Sarah finally talked to him to see where they stood.

Unfortunately, Justin told her that he did not want to be in a serious or committed relationship because he wanted to focus on his work at the firm. He told Sarah that he really liked her and wanted to continue seeing her, but he just could not give her the relationship that she desired. Sarah was very disappointed with Justin's position, but she convinced herself of her own situation just a few years earlier. She thanked Justin for his honesty and told him that she wanted to continue dating him. She was convinced that he would soon fall in love with her and change his mind.

Sarah continued to date Justin for the next several months, and her feelings for him grew stronger. Her desire to be in a committed relationship with him grew stronger as well. Although she refrained most of the time, Sarah occasionally inquired about the status of their relationship. Her questions were always met with the same response from Justin: he did not want a committed relationship and just wanted to take things one day at a time. Fearful of losing him, Sarah accepted what she could get from him, and the couple continued to date. But Sarah was often disappointed by Justin, who frequently cancelled or changed their plans because of work obligations. This became increasingly frustrating for Sarah, who found herself constantly thinking about Justin and whether or not she should continue to date him. And despite her understanding that he didn't want a committed relationship, Sarah did not go out with any other men.

Obviously, this story does not have a happy ending. Despite feeling increasingly dissatisfied with her relationship, Sarah continued to make Justin her number-one priority. Every week, she hesitated to make plans with friends until she could confirm that he was not available. She also found herself cancelling plans with friends if he called her with spur-of-the-moment plans. Sarah was definitely not happy about her relationship with Justin, but she couldn't bring herself to end things with him.

But the relationship did finally come to an end when Sarah's best friend spotted Justin in a restaurant having dinner and holding hands with another woman. Sarah was more than disappointed, she was devastated. She was frustrated with herself and felt as though she had allowed him to take advantage of her patience.

Sarah made a few big mistakes when she started dating Justin. The first mistake happened when Sarah failed to believe what Justin was telling her. He said he didn't want a relationship, but she was convinced that he would eventually change his mind. Sarah also failed to listen to herself. She knew that she wanted a serious and committed relationship, yet she made excuses and tried to fool herself into believing that she could wait for him to be ready. Her dissatisfaction with the relationship was then intensified by her own frustration with herself for putting her life on hold and making Justin a priority over her friends and family.

Many couples struggle with conflicting priorities and get into very similar situations. Here, Sarah made her relationship with Justin her number-one priority. Because she focused on Justin so much, she became more invested in the relationship, and her feelings for him grew stronger. She always made herself available whenever he had time for her. This subconsciously sent the message that she really needed Justin and that her own life wasn't that important. After all, she was willing to take whatever time she could get, even if she had to cancel her plans just to see him. As a result, Justin no longer needed to make Sarah a priority or to work hard to keep her affection.

The lesson is simple: When a person is obsessed with their work or career, developing a relationship might not be a priority. In fact, like Sarah, they may fear that a serious relationship will threaten their ability to achieve their goals.

I'll give you a personal example from my life. I spent most of 2012 on a personal mission to find the love of my life. Being in a committed relationship was a high priority, so I made time to meet, talk to, and go on dates. Today, things are quite different, and I often feel as though I simply don't have enough hours in a day. I am focused on different goals, and I fear that a relationship would take time away from my work. Because of this, I haven't been interested in, talked to, or gone on a date with anyone for at least six months. It wouldn't matter who was pursuing or interested in me. Even if my fairy tale, mirror-match, once-in-a-lifetime, love-of-my-life soul mate were standing right in front of me, I'd still have to pass. I'm sure I'd regret it later, but I'd pass nonetheless.

We make time for people and things that are priorities. If the person you're dating is "too busy," a relationship just might not be an option for them. Their priorities and focus are somewhere else. They might apologize for their lack of time or commitment to you and tell you that you deserve better. When they do, *you should believe them*. Don't take it personally or question whether you're good enough. It is *not* a reflection of you, period.

If you begin dating a person who doesn't make you a high priority, don't waste a moment thinking about their situation or wondering when it might change. Your feelings are important, and you deserve someone who is just as ready and committed as you are. Move forward and find someone who is on the same page as you are. You will be so happy that you did. Remember, if you're busy waiting, wondering, and worrying about the "relationship," you just might miss the opportunity to meet the right one. Because no matter how busy a person is, they will always find time for the things that are most important to them.

Someone you haven't even met is day-dreaming about being in a relationship with a person exactly like YOU!

DATING A PERSON WHO'S ALWAYS LOOKING FOR THE NEXT BEST THING

When you have too many choices, it becomes more difficult to make a selection and feel happy about it. And when it comes to dating and relationships, knowing that these choices exist can potentially make it more difficult for people to commit and stay committed to their partner. Choice overload is definitely a paradox of progress. To further explain how choice overload can make it more difficult for people to commit, allow me to introduce the Investment Model of Relationship Commitment.

In the early 1980s, social psychologist Caryl Rusbult developed the investment model of relationship commitment as a useful theory to explain how and why people become committed to and stick to their partners. According to Rusbult, couples' dependence on and commitment to their relationships is based on three factors:

1. Partners become dependent and committed to relationships when they experience high levels of satisfaction as a result of involvement. Partners are satisfied when their relationships gratify their important needs such as companionship, intimacy, sexuality, and belonging.

2. Partners' dependence and commitment also increases when they believe that the alternatives are less desirable than their current relationship. In other words, if a

person's important needs could be better fulfilled outside of the relationship or if their partner is easily replaced by someone better, then their dependence on the current relationship diminishes.

3. Partners' dependence and commitment is influenced by how much they have invested into the relationship in terms of time, energy, and other important resources. They form deep connections by linking themselves to the relationship in so many ways. Partners who share a home, family, friends, possessions, and income have made these huge investments into the relationship, making it far too costly to break and lose.

With regard to online dating, the seemingly endless catalogue of available singles causes some people to question the choices they make. Believing that they might find a better alternative can make it more difficult for some people to make a commitment, despite the fact that things are going so well. This choice overload often leaves some great clues that are easy to spot.

The most obvious clue that you're dating a person with choice overload is their refusal to hide or take down their online dating profile, even though things seem to be getting more serious between the two of you. If you're feeling like "this is a relationship," then perhaps it's time to have the "Exclusivity Talk" with your new sweetheart. And when two people are in an "exclusive" relationship, neither have any reason to be active on a dating website. So, taking down your online profile seems like the right thing to do.

There are also situations when the person you're dating agrees to take down their dating profile because they want you to do the same. In this case, they are motivated by the fear that you might find a more suitable partner if you're still active online. So, they want to make sure you are "off the market," while they continue to look for "the next best thing," only in a more covert way. This person will certainly leave less obvious clues regarding their dubious ways.

Another clue that your new boyfriend/girlfriend is keeping their options open is when you notice that they avoid posting couple photos of the two of you ... especially if they're otherwise active on social media. New couples who are excited about a future together usually want to share their happiness with friends and family. If that's not happening in your situation, it might be appropriate to inquire about it.

When you're with the person you're supposed to spend your life with, you will know it beyond a shadow of doubt.

- *You might know it immediately,*
- *You might know it after some time, or*
- *You might know it when it's too late!*

13
PLAYERS AND CHEATERS

*Some people are experts at creating attraction,
but failures at creating relationships.*

Remember the Ashley Madison fallout? Hackers posted customer data (names, addresses and sexual fantasies) of 33 million customers who used the online dating service to have an affair. Business for marriage counselors and divorce attorneys should be great for the next year. After all, infidelity is a betrayal and the single most cited cause of divorce.

Without question, infidelity can devastate the individuals in the relationship, their children, and extended family members. Yet despite the consequences, a large percentage of exclusive romantic relationships are affected by it. And for years, psychologists have been trying to find out why.

Researchers investigating unfaithful partners report several motives for infidelity including: relationship dissatisfaction, emotional neglect, anger or revenge, and sexual motives. Except for cases with sexual motives, problems with the primary relationship are blamed for the infidelity. And, outside of the relationship factors, it's impossible to predict who is likely to have an affair? But, we can point out the risk factors that lead to infidelity and may be cause for concern. So, here are five warning signs that your partner might have a cheating heart.

1. THE BEST PREDICTOR OF FUTURE BEHAVIOR IS PAST BEHAVIOR.

As simple as it sounds, past behaviors are the best predictor of future behaviors. History repeats itself, so you need to know your partner's past. Ask questions about relationships, their lengths and level of commitment, and inquire about why the relationships ended. And, don't skip questions about infidelity or their opinions on what is, and what is not appropriate interaction with friends.

A history of past infidelity does not guarantee that infidelity will happen in a current relationship. People learn from their mistakes and experience personal growth. And when they do, they are open to sharing their lessons. But, if your partner responds to your questions with a cavalier attitude, make a mental note of this red flag and further explore this topic. Remember, those who fail to learn from mistakes of the past usually repeat them.

Early in relationships, your beliefs (good and bad) about a partner are more influenced by your imagination than by what your partner shares.

2. CHEATING INTENTIONS

Much of the research on infidelity points to three factors that together influence one's intention to cheat. These factors include having a favorable (blasé) attitude towards infidelity, having a social network that condones or supports infidelity, and having confidence in one's ability to attract a romantic partner. Be careful, red flags are often hidden and not immediately disclosed. This underscores the importance of knowing your partner and sharing the emotional intimacy that develops through trust and feeling safe enough to disclose what's really on your mind.

3. "I LOVE YOU" (LIMITED TIME OFFER, AVAILABLE WHILE PASSIONS LAST)

Serial monogamy is pattern of engaging in several, intense, passionate, and short lived romantic relationships, in a series, one after the other. Serial monogamists are addicted to the thrill and passion of new love and bounce from one person to the next without regard for the pain they inflict. The good news is they are not likely to cheat on their significant other while their relationship is intense and exciting. But when those feelings wane and their attention is drawn elsewhere, they begin a new relationship before the last one ends.

4. THE CASANOVA OR APHRODITE SYNDROME (LUDIC LOVE STYLE)

The Casanova (male) or Aphrodite (female) syndrome is characterized by an obsessive desire to have sex with a variety of different partners without deep emotional investment. These Ludic lovers are players and may have several partners at a time. They regard sex as a sport and engage in relationships as long as it remains a challenge to gain control over their partner

Too often, those who get involved with a Casanova or Aphrodite become convinced of their partners undying love and loyalty and believe their new partner can change. Reality Check- these people rarely change. If he looks like a Casanova and acts like a Casanova, guess what?

5. INVESTMENT MODEL OF RELATIONSHIP COMMITMENT.

In the early 1980s, social psychologist Caryl Rusbult developed the investment model of relationship commitment to explain how people become committed to and stick to their partners. According to the model, couples' commitment to relationships is contingent upon three factors: relationship satisfaction, quality of alternatives, and investments.

Partners' commitment to their relationship increases when they experience high levels of satisfaction of their important needs such as companionship, intimacy, sexuality, and belonging. Commitment is also strengthened by the belief that one is unlikely to find someone better than his or her current partner. Finally, commitment is influenced by how much one has invested into the relationship in terms of time, energy, and other important resources. Homes, family, friends, possessions, and income are huge investments into the relationship and make it far too costly to break and lose. So pay attention to the health and happiness of your relationship and your partner's level of investment. That's the best diagnostic tool you can use to predict infidelity.

Sometimes we fail to get what we 'think' we want because we 'know' we deserve so much more.

HIND SIGHT IS TWENTY-TWENTY

When reflecting on past relationships, people often recognize early warning signs they previously overlooked. Sometimes couples are blinded by love and minimize the red flags they see. Others hide in denial and rationalize bad behavior. Don't let that happen to you. Ask your partner important questions and talk about your feelings. If you find you are hesitant, perhaps you don't yet know your partner well enough to be in a committed relationship.

The most difficult decision you will ever have to make is to walk away from a love you know isn't right for you.

14
CAN FLIRTING BE HARMLESS?

The statement, "Dad, Antonio is performing again" always makes me smile and laugh. It's what Gianna says when she notices her brother Antonio flirting with one of her friends. She uses "performing" instead of "flirting", but make no mistake about it, he's flirting and he's been doing it since he was two or three years old.

The dictionary defines flirting as behaving in a way that shows a sexual attraction for someone but is not meant to be taken seriously. That definition may be accurate for innocent flirting, but we all know that some people have bigger intentions. Many people flirt to explore the potential for a romantic or sexual relationship. And when that happens outside of a committed relationship, the line between innocent fun and intentional infidelity is blurred.

So, why do committed people flirt? When should a committed person (or their partner) become concerned that flirting has gone too far? This chapter explains the various types of flirting and alerts you to four signs that your 'flirting' is 'flirting' with cheating.

FLIRTING- ALWAYS SERVES A PURPOSE

Northern Illinois University professor David Dryden Henningsen, a leading researcher on flirting, offers a comprehensive definition. He defines flirting as ambiguous goal-motivated behaviors that can be, but are not restricted to being, interpreted as sexually motivated. This definition emphasizes flirting's goal-motivated and ambiguous nature as essential characteristics. It's these motivations and intentions that distinguish playful flirting from acts of infidelity. Dr. Henningsen has identified six motivations for flirting as follows:

PLAYFULLY MOTIVATED

This is playful bantering and teasing that's enjoyable to both parties and motivated by fun. It's a harmless and innocent activity that makes neither party uncomfortable.

RELATIONALLY MOTIVATED

Healthy flirting between partners who seek to intensify the intimacy in their relationship.

ESTEEM MOTIVATED

When flirting is well-received and reciprocated it feels good and might boost self-esteem. So, men and women engage in flirting because it is flattering and makes them feel attractive. People also flirt to compliment or make another feel better about themselves.

INSTRUMENTAL MOTIVATION

This is flirting used to persuade someone to do something for you. As one of my friends pointed out, "I might flirt with the bartender to get my drinks quicker, but that doesn't mean I want to go home with him."

EXPLORING MOTIVATION

The ambiguous nature of flirting makes it easy to indirectly convey romantic or sexual interest with a lowered risk of rejection. So, men and women flirt to gauge, test, and explore whether another person is interested in beginning a relationship.

SEXUALLY MOTIVATED

This is flirting motivated by a desire to facilitate sexual contact or a sexual relationship.

WHEN FLIRTING BECOMES CHEATING

Couples have varying degrees of comfort with flirting. The playful bantering among friends that one couple finds amusing is uncomfortable and threatening to another couple. That's why it's important to talk to your partner and agree upon boundaries acceptable to you both. And if either partner violates a promise or commitment you've made to the other, then you have a problem regardless.

It's obvious that flirting motivated by romantic or sexual desires crosses the line into infidelity. But that's not usually the way it begins. Often, flirting begins innocently and progresses, blurring the line between harmless fun and inappropriate behavior. That said, here are four 'not so obvious' signs that flirting has gone too far.

WHEN YOU THINK ABOUT FLIRTING WITH THE SAME PERSON

Let's face it, flirting is fun and can make us feel good. But daydreaming, reminiscing, and looking forward to playful flirtations with one person is a sign that more is developing. Ask yourself this question, "Do you often catch yourself thinking about your flirtatious friend when they're not near you?" If you answer, "Yes", it's time to reevaluate your friendship.

WHEN YOU KEEP YOUR FLIRTATIOUS BEHAVIORS SECRET

If the flirting is kept a secret from your partner, family, friends, and co-workers, ask yourself why? Not telling your sensitive partner about the hunky UPS person you flirt with is one thing. But when you're uncomfortable telling your best friend about your flirting, you've probably crossed the line.

WHEN YOU FEEL GUILT-RIDDEN

Would your partner feel betrayed if they could read your mind and experience your feelings when you are flirting with your friend? Are you guilt-ridden after flirting because you enjoyed it so much? If so, perhaps your friendship is bordering on inappropriate and it's time to stop now.

WHEN YOU SHARE EMOTIONAL INTIMACY

We all need the love, acceptance and appreciation of another person. And when these intimacy needs are not met, we are lonely, regardless of our relationship status. Loneliness is your heart craving for intimacy and connection but having not having anyone willing to connect. This can certainly occur when we are single and alone, but it also occurs in relationships where one or both partners are emotionally unavailable.

Friendly bantering and flirting can get us to open up and share more of our thoughts and emotions. What starts as a playful friendship then becomes the foundation of an emotionally intimate relationship. If you find that you share more of your emotions with your flirtatious friend because they understand you better, you've already moved into dangerous territory.

15
JEALOUSY, MANIPULATION, CONTROL AND ABUSE

No matter how hard you try to make something happen your way, your partner's behavior is never yours to control.

The beginning of a relationship is usually idyllic. Both partners bring their best behavior to the table and lovingly stare into each other's eyes, usually seeing only the positive traits of the other. Sadly, this "honeymoon period" occurs in the beginning of almost all relationships, even those that will turn out to be characterized by jealousy, control, and manipulation.

Jealous partners will usually hold themselves back in the beginning. This is for a couple of reasons. First, that honeymoon period affects them, too. Their new partner is loving, doting, and always available. And they are happy and optimistic that they've found someone who will treat them the way they want.

But there is a darker reason many controlling and abusive personality types hold back. It's a part of their long-term process to manipulate the people who love them. On a first date, the other person has very little time and emotion invested. If the person on the other side of the table demands to read their text messages, it's not hard to get up and walk away. The jealous partner needs to build up the other person's trust and love before showing their more controlling side. These behaviors then grow slowly over time, little things here and there. They test the limits and the boundaries. Eventually they have free reign to act however they like, and the other person does little to nothing to stop them.

For those who are concerned about ending up in this terrible situation, there are warning signs. But they aren't easy to spot. You have to be looking for them and always on the alert. And it's this very requirement to be suspicious that stops someone from noticing those red flags. Most people are trusting by nature, because we want to believe the best in other people. If someone has been caught in a jealousy-filled relationship, they are more adept at spotting the signs and running to higher ground. But someone who hasn't been hurt like this (and that's most people), it feels almost wrong to analyze their new partner's every move. It's as if they are a bad person because they are looking for evil in someone they've begun to care about. They often tell themselves that they're just sabotaging their own happiness and they need to shake it off and enjoy the new relationship.

But that is the problem. It's these people, the fundamentally good, trusting people, who are at the highest risk. The jealous, controlling people are looking for them because they know they can ease into their manipulative behaviors and won't experience any push back: *"Maybe he speaks disrespectfully about his ex, but she probably really hurt him or he just wants to assure me there's nothing there to rekindle."* Or, *"She never accepts responsibility when something is her fault, no matter how small it is. Maybe she's been in a relationship where everything was blamed on her and she's sensitive about it now. I should be more supportive; her mistakes have been so small anyway."*

Other big warning signs include lavishing a new partner with gifts, especially when that partner is comfortable with all the showiness. This creates a foundation where any complaint by the new partner brings accusations of ungratefulness and greediness: *"After all I've done for you, this is what I get?"*

And it's not just about how they treat their new partner. Warning signs are often evident by the way they treat everyone else. The waiter brings the wrong wine and it turns into a scene where the manager is called. Someone bumps into him on the street and he yells obscenities even though he wasn't harmed in the slightest. She makes critical comments about every other woman in the room, not caring who hears her. These people typically have short tempers and work the hardest at hiding it in their treatment of the new partner. But they hide it less when it comes to strangers, so it can be seen earlier. It can also be exposed while in a group setting. Maybe jokes are made at the expense of you or other people in your party and everyone laughs, but it's really not a joke you're comfortable with. These situations are also testing grounds for more controlling behaviors because the new partner is less likely to argue when there are other people around.

The hardest warning sign to acknowledge is how quickly things progress. She wants to go out every night. He wants to move in after a month. In our society, we typically equate this with a fairy tale. We're tired of people with commitment issues and someone who is willing to say "I love you" and talk marriage and children seems to be a rare creature who must be cherished. The jealous partner may claim they're just perfect for each other, that it was love at first sight, and other romantic-sounding things. Unfortunately, the desirability of this behavior gives jealous partners the best opportunity to gain total control over the other partner's schedule and life.

As things progress and get more serious, we see new signs developing. One is finding out that the partner has unrealistic expectations. They want the Disney relationship, often with very stereotypical gender roles. He should be providing, and if his job isn't going well, there's a problem. She should keep the house, and if dinner isn't on the table when he gets home, there's a problem. Their entire happiness is bluntly placed on their partner. It doesn't matter what else is going on in life, if their partner isn't living up to expectations then the world might as well be coming to an end. You are their world, after all.

Another sign is hypersensitivity. This refers to the jealous partner overreacting to little things: comments, jokes, or small issues. These people often have low self-esteem and tend to take everything personally. They may be easily insulted or claim that the world is against them if they encounter a slight setback. If you disagree about anything, no matter how trivial, you're insulting them to their core and calling them a terrible person who can't do anything right. This often shows itself in a set of rules that have a clear double standard. If she seems to glance at another man, then she clearly doesn't find her partner attractive anymore and is cheating on him. But if she comments on him blatantly staring at other women, then she is calling him a pervert and accusing him of terrible things he would never do.

These are just some of the early warning signs that your partner has a controlling, mistrusting disposition. Each person expresses it differently, but these are among the most common and more easily noted. And observing this only one time doesn't mean you should run for the hills. But if you're seeing multiple warning signs or a progressive pattern begin to develop, then there may be cause for concern. Paying close attention to how your partner acts and treats you does not make you a bad person, it makes you a wise person who is protecting themselves. At the end of the day, trust your instincts. If something doesn't sound or feel right, take note of it and do what's best for you and what will keep you safe.

Letting go and walking away from a toxic relationship is heart-wrenching and painful; it's also uniquely empowering and life changing.

16
DECIPERING THEIR CHANGE OF HEART

If they walk away without a reason, don't let them return with an excuse!

Why is dating so difficult? When you like someone, you show them and hope to receive the same level of attention in return. That's how dating should be, right? But too often, things are different. You get excited and hopeful about a person you're dating, then they change and leave you wondering if they are still interested. We gauge our interactions, share our stories with friends and resign to the conclusion that "It's complicated."

Sometimes things start off great, then suddenly shift in the wrong direction. A friend who frequently texts or calls now inconsistently responds to you. The concerned guy who made plans now cancels dates at the last minute. And, let's not forget about the short, one or two word responses to your attempts at conversing through text. Yes, their behavior change is easy to spot and produces uneasy and uncertain feelings about the relationship. If you're anything like me, you're left wondering what caused their change of heart.

IT'S NOT ALWAYS ABOUT YOU

New relationships are fragile and exploratory. Despite promising beginnings, it's not uncommon for one (or both) partners to experience a sudden change of heart. Sometimes, the reason is obvious. But when it's not, you're left puzzled, confused and anxious for answers. Did I do something wrong? Was it something I said? Did I seem too needy or clingy? Or, does someone else have their attention?

A sudden change of heart without an obvious reason is often a triggered emotional response. Some behavior, interaction or new information triggered a negative emotion in your partner and caused them to experience anxiety. This uneasiness gets associated with you, and poof, they're gone. Unless you were offensive, or made an awkward faux pas, the trigger is related to something in your partner's past and has nothing to do with you. A trigger could be almost anything: behaviors, gestures, expressions, differences of opinion, or even the way you laugh.

Sometimes a trigger is an alert to important differences between two people. But often, a trigger is simply an irrational emotional response to something your partner isn't even aware of. So, don't blame yourself or spend endless hours worrying about what went wrong. It happens to everyone, it happens frequently and it's not a reflection of you. Period!

BUT SOMETIMES IT IS ABOUT YOU

Let's face it — sometimes people need a reality check. If you get more than your fair share of rejection, it may be time for a self-evaluation. Did you turn your partner off? Perhaps a joke you made was misconstrued or misinterpreted. Or, were you drinking or smoking cigarettes on the date? Something as simple as a difference in lifestyle could explain everything. That's not to suggest that you shouldn't be yourself. You should be! In fact, it is essential you be true to yourself and not compromise your feelings and values to be the "perfect partner."

So, conduct an in-depth probe of your personality, attitude, and behavior. There may be ways you need to change. For most, an honest self-evaluation will reveal the problem, but some people will struggle to recognize how they sabotage their success with potential dates. If that's your experience, enlist the help of a professional dating coach or relationship therapist. Doing so might be the most effective way to turn your dating dilemmas into dating delight!

Remember, anyone who is dating will have these experiences and it won't feel good. What's important is that you quickly recognize when your feelings are no longer being reciprocated—and once you're aware, adjust your behaviors and feelings accordingly. Don't waste your time worrying about the person who isn't showing as much interest as you are. Move forward and meet someone as eager about a relationship as you are. Don't settle for anything less. You deserve a person who's excited about you and knows how to show it.

17
SO YOU'VE BEEN GHOSTED: HERE ARE SIX STEPS TO DEAL WITH IT

Goodbye is not the opposite of hello;
both pave the way to new beginnings.

Breaking-up with a person who likes you is never easy. It usually requires having an awkward 'break-up' talk that is especially difficult when your partner doesn't see it coming. But guess what? There's an app for that!

Yes, you read that correctly. Binder is an iOS and Android app that offers a relationship-ending service. Simply enter your partner's name and phone number, and choose from a list of reasons, and Binder does the "Binning" (break-up calls and texts) for you. It's brutally honest and to the point.

While using an app to dump someone is impersonal, a more heartless route is the increasingly common act of ghosting! Ghosting is the process of ending a romantic (or platonic) relationship by cutting off, blocking, or ignoring your former partner's attempts to contact you. Basically, when you're ghosting someone, you're ending a relationship without acknowledging, explaining, or informing your partner of your intentions.

Being ghosted Sucks! It leaves you confused, frustrated, and disrespected as you search for clues to explain the disappearance. And, if you've ever been ghosted you know how unsettling it can be. Here are five steps to help you get over your unfriendly ghost.

1. RECOGNIZE YOU'VE BEEN GHOSTED

One of the worst aspects of ghosting is the fact that it might take some time before you realize that you've been faded-out. While you're waiting for a response, you'll question whether the other person got your texts or saw your missed calls. Communication failures happen all the time, so it's possible your partner thought they responded, but you never received the message.

Make a friendly phone call or send a brief message checking on them and remind them you had tried to make contact. If you still don't hear from them within a few days, it's time to accept the fact you're being ghosted.

2. ACCEPTANCE

Coping with the end of a romantic relationship is never an easy process. But when you're ghosted, it's more difficult because you may hang on to false hope. And without accepting that it's over, you might engage in behaviors focused on getting your ex back and prolong your suffering. The process of recovering begins with accepting that it has happened. Acceptance allows the healing to begin and facilitates a quicker recovery from the disappointment.

3. NO HUNTING AND HAUNTING

Hunting involves going to places with a high probability of running into an ex-partner. In doing so, the Hunter fantasizes that their ex-partner will have a sudden and dramatic change of heart after a 'coincidental' meeting. Haunting refers to stalking behaviors like driving by the ex-partner's home or monitoring their social media sites hoping to see that nothing in their life has changed.

These hunting and haunting behaviors are detrimental to your recovery for several reasons. First, they require you to spend considerable time and energy thinking about your ex-partner and what they might be doing. And when you find evidence that your ex-partner has moved on, you'll make unfavorable comparisons to your life and ruminate about your loss. Too often, the information you learn is incomplete, and you become more curious. Again, the focus is on your ex, instead of focusing on things you could do to speed up your recovery.

4. SEEK UNDERSTANDING, IF POSSIBLE

If you're single and dating, chances are you've been ghosted. And when it happens to you, you are left wondering what happened. It's important to remember that people ghost because they want to avoid confrontation or conflict. The lazy ghost hopes the problem will just go away if they avoid the other person forever.

Of course, your partner's avoidance leaves you wondering what provoked their change of heart in the first place. Let's face it, sometimes the reason for the relationship's end is clear. Perhaps there was a disagreement or dispute leading to your partner's decision to bail out. If so, ask yourself the tough questions and have the courage to answer them honestly. Perhaps you did something or said something that alienated your partner and contributed to the breakup. Assess these behaviors and why they occurred. Were they situational behaviors, habitual behaviors, or personality characteristics?

An understanding of the behaviors and personality characteristics that led to conflict allows you to learn from the experience. Perhaps you recognize how you could have behaved differently. Or was the conflict a result of your partner's objection to a belief of yours. In that case, you'll realize that you would do the exact same thing again and conclude that your personalities are incompatible.

5. IT'S NOT ABOUT YOU AT ALL

Sometimes the decision to end a relationship is not about you. Technology makes meeting people easier than ever. Mobile and online dating, provides an endless catalogue of available singles. And when you have too many options, it becomes more difficult to choose and be happy about it. Knowing that these choices exist might make it more difficult for people to commit and stay committed to their partner. Ghosting is also common when an 'on-again, off-again ex' shows up asking for another chance. Or, perhaps your partner was dating other people and things became more serious with one of them.

These explanations don't justify ghosting or make it an acceptable way to end a relationship. But, they do lessen your burden. If there wasn't an obvious disagreement or falling-out that you regret, go easy on yourself, it's not about you!

6. FOCUS ON YOU AND DON'T LOSE HOPE

After being ghosted, many people engage in 'desperation dating' and frantically search for their next date. Indeed, rebounding can take the focus off of your ghost, but accepting an undesirable but available new partner could be even worse. Instead, focus on being a better you and enjoying your extra time with friends and family. Be single like Prince Harry: happily eligible until someone equally amazing wins your heart.

18
DATING AND RELATIONSHIP RULES

Relationships are NOT made in heaven. They come in "individual" kits that take time and effort to put together.

Every new relationship is ignited by sparks of interest, allure, and a desire to be near one another. This attraction can be physical, sexual, emotional, or a combination of all of them and results in what many people call "chemistry". When we feel this chemistry with another person, we know it, and the feeling is unmistakable. The outcome of the couples' chemistry depends on their circumstances, availability, and most of all, how the two choose to interact with one another.

We have all had the experience of being very excited about someone who likes us, only to find that they have experienced a sudden change of heart and end the friendship. More often than not, something related to your interaction together triggered some anxiety or familiar feeling in your partner. That's not to imply that you did something wrong, as long as your behavior wasn't intentionally offensive. Triggers are often related to something in your partner's past, have nothing to do with you, and should never be taken personally. It happens to everyone, and it happens frequently.

Understanding why a person "just isn't that into you" is like understanding why you prefer vanilla ice cream over chocolate. You'll never know the reason and it shouldn't matter anyway.

One can never predict or control how a person is going to react to something we say or do. Instead, we can only do our best to communicate our thoughts and feelings and hope the receiver understands. But when we remain silent and fail to express ourselves, we may be communicating something unintentionally. These unspoken messages often communicate bad things like... "It's OK for you to treat me that way", "My opinion doesn't matter", "My time isn't as important as yours; I'm willing to accept any time I can have with you" etc.

Clearly, our interaction with our partner can mean the difference between a blossoming relationship and one that fails to get past the first date. That's not to suggest that you shouldn't be yourself. You should be! In fact, it is essential that you be true to yourself and not compromise your feelings and values in an attempt to be the "perfect partner". And when we really like someone, it becomes easier to stray off of the path we have made for ourselves.

I have worked with thousands of people who struggle with dating and relationship issues. While their faces and names are different, the types of issues and problems they face are the same. I'll get the identical question from a woman in Malaysia as from a woman in

California. So, it becomes easy to predict their outcomes should they choose to continue doing what they've always done. Still, the people that I work with are often amazed that what I told them was exactly how things panned out.

Over the years, I have come up with stories and scenarios that I share to help people understand some of the more common relationship issues. Eventually, these stores went through a reduction process and have been condensed into quotes and Tweets. I've collected many of my favorites and present them in the form of "Dating and Relationship Rules".

Like most things in life, an amazing relationship is also based on some principles and rules. Some of these "Rules" have been written in the form of a directive to follow, while the others are written as rules that you should never break. Following these rules will put you on the path to developing a healthy and loving relationship. But beware, while they may seem to be simple common sense, staying true to these rules requires dedication and effort, especially when you are really into a new relationship.

RULE #1
KNOW THYSELF, LOVE THYSELF, AND RESPECT THYSELF FIRST, ONLY THEN CAN YOU BE READY FOR A PARTNER TO DO THE SAME.

This is the first and most important rule, because if you practice Relationship Rule #1, you can expect that most of the other rules will be practiced as well. We stress the importance of knowing yourself—your values, desires, likes, and dislikes that impact relationships because they are the pre-requisites for knowing what you value and appreciate in a partner. Likewise, knowing what you cannot tolerate in a partner is equally important in helping to spot incompatibility early on. Loving and respecting yourself as your own best friend, means that you can be your true self without compromising your values or beliefs in the hopes of winning over your partner. Hiding your true self behind a fabricated "perfect partner personality" may temporarily impress your partner, but it will ultimately result in experiencing feelings of resentment, disappointment, and anger.

RULE #2
KNOW YOUR PARTNER (THEN YOU CAN*), LOVE YOUR PARTNER, AND RESPECT YOUR PARTNER.

We learn about our partners and grow closer to them on an emotional level when we spend "relationship time" sharing and communicating with them intimately. We develop emotional intimacy by knowing a person's ideas, desires, and feelings about themselves as well as their thoughts and feelings about us. And, emotional intimacy can only develop between people who trust one another and feel safe enough to disclose what's really on their mind.

Having said that, when couples are hesitant to ask each other important questions or talk about their true feelings, then they aren't ready to commit to one another other because they lack trust and don't know each other well enough. Often, couples in new relationships share far more sexual intimacy than emotional intimacy. They get to know each other's bodies and sexual preferences far better and earlier than understanding who they are emotionally.

When reflecting on past relationships, people are able to recognize early warning signs, red-flags, or behaviors that expose some undisclosed or hidden aspect of their partner's personality, attitudes, and intentions. While these "red-flags" may be obvious to outsiders, they are often overlooked for a number of reasons. Sometimes couples are blinded by the excitement of love. Others hide in denial and minimize the severity of the behavior and believe it's an isolated incidence. And finally, some partners think they can cope with a particular behavior or believe that the person will change.

It is during these times that being your own best friend is most important. Best friends want to protect us and have our best interest at heart. They will point out red-flags and warning signs and insist that you take your time in getting to know your partner before investing too much into the relationship making it more difficult to unravel.

RULE #3

SAY WHAT YOU FEEL AND MEAN WHAT YOU SAY!

When you need something from your partner, ask for it. Never assume or expect that your partner should know what you are thinking or what you really meant. No one can read your mind, nor can anyone always anticipate your needs. If you want your partner's attention, affection, time, or consideration... ask for it. Being upfront with your true feelings will save you from preventable conflicts. If you are fearful of sharing your needs with your partner, then your relationship is lacking intimacy and TRUST.

RULE #4

LISTEN WITH YOUR EYES! THE BEST EVIDENCE OF WHAT PEOPLE TRULY FEEL AND BELIEVE COMES NOT FROM THEIR WORDS BUT FROM THEIR ACTIONS.

In all relationships we communicate simultaneously on at least two levels; what we say, and what we do. Usually, a person's behavior and words are consistent and convey the same message. But sometimes, a person's behavior and words convey different messages making them difficult to comprehend and harder to trust. And, dating a person like this is frustrating and unsatisfying. Nevertheless, some people elect to believe the communication that best suits their needs. For example, some men and women will continue dating a person who repeatedly promises to change a behavior but never delivers. Others will continue dating a person who claims they don't want a commitment, yet they want to behave like a couple and reap the benefits of a relationship. The person wanting the commitment chooses to ignore what they are told in favor of what they want to believe. This ultimately results in feeling resentment, frustration and fosters a relationship void of honesty, emotional intimacy, and trust. Make sure the person you choose to date is communicating the same message with both their words and their actions.

RULE #5

PUTTING A PARTNER'S NEEDS FIRST CAN BE A BEAUTIFUL GIFT, BUT ONLY BETWEEN PARTNERS WHO ARE ABLE TO SHARE EQUALLY IN THE GIVING AND RECEIVING.

People who constantly put the needs of their partner first often believe they're being unselfish and honorable. After all, if they devote so much of their time and energy to their significant other's life, then that makes them a wonderful partner, right?

The hope is that if you put your lover's wishes and needs first, they will fall deeply in love with you and begin to treat you the same. You justify the behavior as selfless, loving, and ideal, so you continue to put yourself last. And because you want to be "unselfish," you simply wait for your partner to reciprocate.

Assuming that your partner will anticipate or ask about your desires (like you have) will usually backfire and leave you feeling disappointed, neglected, or taken advantage of. Because you have invested so much more time and energy into the relationship, you begin to feel that you love your partner more than they love you, and your partner begins to sense your "neediness."

Remember the Investment Model -- We tend to like, appreciate, depend, and commit to the things (and people) that we have invested in. So, your partner's dependence and commitment is also influenced by how much they have invested into the relationship in terms of time, energy, and other important resources. Let your partner invest in you; they will appreciate you more as a result. Better yet, invest in each other equally—share in the giving and receiving and you will both be more satisfied.

RULE #6

LOSE THE PERSON WHO WON'T COMMIT BECAUSE THEY ARE "AFRAID OF GETTING HURT". REPLACE THEM WITH SOMEONE WHO IS "AFRAID OF LOSING YOU."

People often come up with excuses for the people who aren't willing to commit. "They are gun-shy after being hurt in their last relationship." Or, "He needs time before he's ready to get serious again." Sound familiar?

Certainly it's appropriate to learn from our experiences and to be cautious with whom we give our hearts to. At the same time, when you meet that one special person who turns your world upside down, you're willing to do whatever it takes to keep that person in your life. Whatever fears you might have won't come close to the fear of losing the one you really love. If a person won't commit because they are "afraid of getting hurt," then move on and find the one that's afraid of losing you.

RULE #7

STOP MAKING EXCUSES FOR THEM! NO MATTER HOW "BUSY" A PERSON IS, IF THEY CARE, THEY WILL ALWAYS FIND TIME FOR YOU.

No matter how busy a person is, if you or your relationship is important and a high priority, they will find the time or make the time for you. If they don't make the time, a relationship just might not be priority.

Don't take it personally or question whether you're good enough. It's not a reflection of you, period. Don't make excuses and fool yourself into believing that you can wait it out. The more thought and energy you invest while waiting, the stronger your feelings will become. So, don't waste another moment thinking about their situation or wondering when it might change. Your feelings are important, and you deserve someone who is just as ready and committed as you are. Move forward and find someone who is on the same page as you are. You will be so happy that you did.

Remember, if you're busy waiting, wondering, and worrying about the "relationship," you just might miss the opportunity to meet the right one.

RULE #8

DON'T BE ANYONE'S SOCIAL MEDIA SECRET! COUPLES WHO WANT A FUTURE TOGETHER ARE EXCITED TO TAKE "COUPLE PHOTOS" TO SHARE WITH FRIENDS.

Does the person you're dating avoid posting photos of the two of you together? Is that person otherwise active on social media? If yes, have you two discussed this? New couples who are excited about a future together usually want to share their happiness with friends and family. If that's not happening in your situation, you should certainly have a conversation about it?

RULE #9

FORGET ABOUT "MIXED MESSAGES." IF A PERSON WANTS YOU, THEY WILL MAKE IT KNOWN BEYOND ANY SHADOW OF DOUBT.

In all relationships, we communicate simultaneously on at least two levels; what we say, and what we do. Usually, a person's verbal and actual behaviors convey the same message. Mixed messages are inconsistencies in communication, where a person may say one thing, but act on another. Getting mixed messages from a person you really like makes them difficult to understand, and harder to trust.

Sometimes, partners enter a relationship with different goals in mind. One person invests in the relationship in hopes of a formal commitment, while the other begins more casually and refuses to make a formal commitment. Still, they act like a couple and reap all the benefits of a relationship. The partner who wants the commitment refuses to accept what they are being told in favor of what they want to believe. Don't get caught up in this arrangement, especially if a long term relationship is what you want. Doing so ultimately results in feelings of resentment and frustration and fosters a relationship void of honesty, emotional intimacy, and trust. Make sure the person you're dating shares your plans for the future and communicates a consistent message with both their words and their actions.

People don't send mixed messages. We only use that to excuse their disappointing behavior. When a person wants to be with someone, they make it crystal clear. When you're getting mixed messages, that's a message in itself.

RULE #10

COUPLES CANNOT RELY ON THEIR MEMORIES ALONE; THEY MUST KEEP THE RELATIONSHIP FRESH IN THE PRESENT AND DEVELOP FUTURE GOALS.

Maintaining closeness and "being on the same page" is critically important to the success of every long term relationship. Without closeness, couples can drift apart and become more susceptible to affairs. Schedule weekly "relationship-time" in the form of date nights where you have each other's undivided attention and focus. This is not the same as simply being in the same house together or running errands together. This "relationship-time" is to focus on your friendship, enjoying one another, communicating, and building intimacy.

RULE #11

BEWARE OF PEOPLE WHO MAY BE HIDING THEIR TRUE SELVES.

Some people can be very good actors who have imitated the actions and behaviors of people in loving relationships. They can create an illusion of intimacy as they seduce you into trusting and loving them. Things are amazing for a while, and then something happens that causes you to question everything. Usually, some trivial issue will trigger an **unbelievably bizarre overreaction** from your partner and leave you feeling completely confused. This is often the first sign that there is something very wrong with your relationship, and that the person you committed to, is not the same person in front of you.

RULE #12

ARE YOU DATING SOMEONE WHO HAS COME ON STRONG AND DEVELOPED FEELINGS FOR YOU VERY QUICKLY? CAUTION! THOSE FEELINGS OFTEN DIE EVEN FASTER.

Relationships that start at blazing speeds are often propelled by a partner who is "needy" in some way. They approach dating their new friend in an almost obsessive way and are quick to express their intense feelings. Be careful! As soon as let your guard down and begin to reciprocate, you may be in for a surprise. Often they will experience a change of heart and end the relationship. Without warning, they disappear, leaving you puzzled about what went wrong.

RULE #13

STAYING IN AN UNHEALTHY RELATIONSHIP TOO LONG WILL MAKE A ONCE HEALTHY PARTNER UNHEALTHY!

Most people know that worry and stress from a toxic relationship can have devastating effects on both physical health and emotional well-being. But did you ever stop to think about what that stress and frustration is doing to your other relationships? What about your job? Has it also crippled your ability to excel at work or in school? Ask yourself: Is it worth it?

RULE #14

IF THEIR "EX" IS REALLY JUST A FRIEND, THEY SHOULD BE YOUR FRIEND TOO.

Sharing your life with someone involves developing relationships with your partner's friends and family. Old friends who want to maintain a relationship with your partner should want to befriend you too, right? If your partner wants to maintain a separate friendship with their ex-partner, you must question their motives and the appropriateness of their friendship.

New relationships should be exciting, passionate, and easy. When you really like someone, you want them to know how valuable and important the relationship is. And, you want to know that your feelings are reciprocated — so, you treat them with as much affection and consideration as you can.

That is exactly how you should be treated in return. Don't settle for anything less. Remember, if you're busy waiting, wondering, and worrying about this relationship, you just might miss the opportunity to meet the right one

RULE #15

NEVER ALLOW ANYONE TO DENY YOUR RIGHT TO YOUR FEELINGS. IF YOU ARE FEELING HURT, IT'S PROBABLY BECAUSE SOMEONE HAS DONE SOMETHING THAT HURT YOU.

If your partner has done something disappointing or hurtful, you don't need a third party to acknowledge your right to be upset. If you feel hurt, your partner should acknowledge your pain and seek to understand you. Beware of anyone who minimizes or ridicules something that hurt you.

RULE #16

DON'T WASTE A MOMENT WORRYING ABOUT THE PERSON WHO DOESN'T CONSISTENTLY RETURN YOUR TEXTS OR CALLS! YOU DESERVE BETTER, SO JUST FORGET THEM AND MOVE ON.

When a person is excited about a new relationship, they tend to check for texts or messages more frequently to be certain that they haven't missed any communication from the person they're dating. I know that I do this and I also keep my "read receipt" on to let the sender know when I've read their message. When you're excited about and like someone, you definitely don't want to disappoint them. That is exactly how you should be treated in return. Don't settle for anything less. You deserve a person who's just as excited about you and eagerly checks their phone in hopes of seeing your texts and messages.

RULE #17

MAKE TIME FOR THE RELATIONSHIPS AND FRIENDS YOU HAD BEFORE YOUR RELATIONSHIP.

Some couples get so wrapped up in each other that they isolate themselves and begin to completely neglect their relationships with other people. Don't neglect or drop the friends who were with you before your relationship. Your friendships are part of who you are... giving them up will lead to feelings of resentment and neglect and foster too much dependence on your partner. If your relationship comes to an end, who will you turn to for support?

RULE #18

DON'T KEEP SECRETS! BREAK-UPS OFTEN BEGIN WITH A PERSON KEEPING A SECRET FROM THEIR PARTNER. ONCE ONE STARTS KEEPING SECRETS, WHERE DOES ONE END.

As a relationship grows, couples become increasingly emotionally intimate and develop trust as they share more and more of themselves. Feeling that you must hide aspects of your current life is sign of problems with your relationship. Perhaps you are doing things that are incongruent with your relationship or you have not yet developed enough trust to share with your partner. Either way, reevaluating your relationship might be wise.

RULE #19

JEALOUS FEELINGS ARE NOT EQUAL TO JEALOUS BEHAVIORS. THE FIRST IS CAUSED BY INSECURITY, THE SECOND BY CONTROL AND POSSESSIVENESS.

Jealousy is an emotion experienced as thoughts and feelings of insecurity, fear, and anxiety over the possibility of losing some human connection or relationship of great personal value. When threated by a rival who expresses interest in our partner, experiencing some jealousy can be a healthy sign of love and a reminder of the value of the relationship. But in the absence of any real threat, a partner expressing jealousy, anger, and disgust may be motivated by possessiveness and a need to control. Learn to recognize the difference.

A partner who is suffocating you by always wanting to be together may be showing early signs of jealous behavior. And, if your partner is offended when you suggest having a night with your friends, you may want to step back and reconsider the relationship.

RULE #20

RELATIONSHIPS ARE NOT MADE IN HEAVEN. THEY COME IN INDIVIDUAL KITS THAT TAKE TIME AND EFFORT TO PUT TOGETHER.

Indeed, all relationships have their own unique set of challenges and problems. Overcoming and solving these challenges requires listening, empathy and negotiation skills. And problems are not always going to be easy to overcome. But the strongest predictor of relationship success, by far, is the desire to make the relationship work, regardless of challenges.

SOME FINAL WORDS FROM ANTONIO

When Theresa agreed to co-write *Dating 2.0* with me, I knew that we were embarking on an emotional rollercoaster that would be unlike anything we had faced before. I was certain that we would disagree on many things and that we would have arguments and fights. After all, being married to one another for ten years, we had become very good at disagreeing and arguing, right? Indeed, we did have more than a few battles about the focus of the book, the content, and even the title and cover art. Nevertheless, I knew that we would always find a way to iron out our differences, and we did.

With Theresa as a trusted co-writer, I expected that our book would have the benefit of both a male and female perspective. During the writing and editing process, these differences became obvious and caused some debate, and some arguments. But mostly, combining our different views caused a lot of laughter. I am proud that our book combines our two perspectives.

Co-writing a relationship book with my ex-wife also made me reminisce about many of the amazing, wonderful and life changing experiences that we've been blessed with. It also forced me to relive every painful mistake and issue I struggled with during our relationship. Indeed, I spent much of my time remembering the thoughts, feelings and motivations that accompanied my past experiences. The process was often challenging and painful, but it definitely furthered my understanding of myself as an individual, as a father, and as a psychologist.

I've argued that knowing yourself and being able to listen to your inner voice in the absence of blinding self-deception are essential pre-requisites for a healthy and happy relationship. That's why so much of the book is concerned with developing and practicing self-love and being your own best friend. But once this friendship is solid, you can't simply rest on your laurels. Best friends cannot rely on their memories alone. Instead, they must tend to that relationship, keep it fresh in the present, and develop future goals. I've recently learned this first hand and it leads me to explain the most important and unanticipated consequence of writing this book.

For the past year, I have been writing this book while also living it. I've diligently followed my own advice and have worked through all of the things that I've suggested to my readers. So, I've recently spent a great deal of time getting to know myself again. And in doing so, I have reacquainted and reconnected with my own best friend --- Antonio. Yes, I got to really know and love the new Antonio: A divorced father of two children. Thankfully, he is a lot like the old Antonio, so we are going to get along well.

I hope that this book was helpful to you. I hope that it has incited in you the courage to believe that you will find life-long love. And,

Some Final Words from Antonio

I hope our book has encouraged you to spend more time practicing self-love. I'm grateful that it has had that effect on me. Perhaps that was the real reason for wanting to write this in the first place.

As we wind down towards my final words, I want to distill all of my thoughts and feelings about this book in one final sentence.

__Know yourself, love yourself, and believe in yourself first, only then can you be ready for a partner to do the same.__

SOME FINAL WORDS FROM THERESA

When Antonio asked me to collaborate on this book, I thought he was joking and told him he was "crazy". And, as he assured me that he was serious, I began trying to come up with reasons—excuses why it was a bad idea. Although I knew it was a tall order, I really couldn't think of any reason why I shouldn't take on the challenge. We had recently redefined our relationship and we were working on building our parenting friendship. Plus, we were both "learning how to date" again, so the topic was certainly relevant for me.

From married at the Vatican to divorced in Detroit, our marriage relationship looped 180 degrees and now we were embarking on this new partnership, a relationship that was yet to be tested. So, I agreed to start writing, but warned him that I would walk away from the book if it threatened our fragile friendship.

My decision to co-write this book with Antonio was based on a few important things. First, we had both experienced the three sides of the same relationship, yet we certainly held differing opinions regarding how and why things started, progressed, and ended the way they did. Perhaps writing a relationship book together could lead us to a better understanding of how the other experienced our lives. I know that co-writing Dating 3.0 has done that for me. For that, I am endlessly grateful.

I suppose I was also ready to face the fact that I was a newbie on today's dating scene and realized I had a very high learning curve to climb. I figured that if we applied our academic backgrounds in psychology with the new experiences we were living every day, we could write a great dating and relationship book that has both a male and female perspective.

We realized that dating has changed so much in the last decade—not knowing the unwritten rules can be very intimidating. Our aim was to shed some light on these unwritten rules and flatten the learning curve for others who are single again and new to dating in the age of social media and the mobile web. I hope that our book has done that for you.

Perhaps most importantly, the completion of this book is a testament to our persistent and stubborn belief that a divorce doesn't have to be tragic and destructive. For many families, divorce means the ending of a marriage and the beginning of a happy family. Antonio and I may have different beliefs and disagree on many issues, but we have always agreed on two principles that are most important to us—We will always be a "family" and nothing is more important than "family".

ABOUT THE AUTHORS

ANTONIO BORRELLO PH.D.

Dr. Antonio Borrello is a nationally recognized psychologist and relationship expert and co-author of Dating 3.0. Antonio is passionate about inspiring others to find and develop life-long relationships that are filled with love, friendship, and mutual respect while embracing the shared goals of building a life together. Dr. Antonio Borrello has worked with thousands of people to improve and heal their most important relationships. He practices in Bloomfield Hills, Michigan and online as a relationship coach. Antonio takes the most pride in his role of "Daddy" to Gianna and Antonio. Join him on Twitter, Instagram, and other social media as @eDatingDr.

THERESA PAVONE, PH.D.

As an inspiring author and an Industrial and Organizational Psychologist Theresa Pavone prides herself on improving relationships in the workplace with effective coaching and work-life balance. Theresa has spent the last 20 years as a Professor and working with Inc. 500 companies. She has authored and published several works. Her greatest accomplishment is her role as the mother of her two children Gianna and Antonio.